EJECT!
THE COMPLETE HISTORY OF
U.S. AIRCRAFT ESCAPE SYSTEMS

EJECT!

THE COMPLETE HISTORY OF U.S. AIRCRAFT ESCAPE SYSTEMS

JIM TUTTLE

MBI Publishing Company

First published in 2002 by MBI Publishing Company, Galtier Plaza,
Suite 200, 380 Jackson Street, St. Paul, MN 55101-3885 USA

MBI Publishing Company books are also available at discounts in bulk
quantity for industrial or sales-promotional use. For details write to
Special Sales Manager at Motorbooks International Wholesalers &
Distributors, Galtier Plaza, Suite 200, 380 Jackson Street, St. Paul, MN
55101-3885 USA.

Library of Congress Cataloging-in-Publication Data Available
ISBN 0-7603-1185-4

On the front cover: A Douglas Aircraft Advanced Concept Ejection
Seat (ACES II) in a zero altitude/zero speed test. Note that even
though the ejection seat is still being powered by its rocket catapult,
the drogue chute is in its deployment sequence. *Douglas Aircraft*

On the back cover: Looking down into the three crew stations of the
Convair B-58 Hustler bomber, the upper surface of the three Stanley
Aviation encapsulated ejection seats are visible.
Convair, via Lockheed Martin

Edited by Chad Caruthers
Designed by LeAnn Kuhlmann

Printed in China

CONTENTS

INTRODUCTION

While the first thoughts of a parachute came from China, it was Leonardo de Vinci who in 1495 first put such thoughts to paper. Subsequently, the first manned balloons stimulated the parachute's practical development, with one of the world's first successful parachute jumps recorded on October 22, 1797, from a balloon at an altitude of about 3,000 feet. Frenchman André-Jacques Garnerin descended into Paris with a rather primitive device—a parachute that appeared more like a parasol.

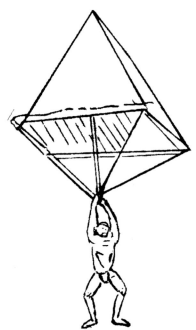

Leonardo de Vinci parachute drawing (1495).

INTRODUCTION

Because parachutes were developed so much earlier than powered aircraft, one might assume that from the beginning of aircraft, parachutes played a role in escaping ailing airplanes. This isn't the case.

Many early aircraft were pusher-types, with whirling propellers directly in the path of a pilot needing to bail out. In addition, there was a myriad of wire bracing and wing struts used in these craft. To bail out would have required an airman to virtually thread himself through this maze to safely exit the aircraft—an impossible task. In addition, the reliability of parachutes was not what it is today. The pack-type parachute had not been perfected and there was little assurance that an inflated parachute would follow the pull of the ripcord. And, of course, early aircraft didn't attain sufficient altitude to allow a parachute canopy the necessary time or distance to inflate and slow a crewman to a safe landing speed.

Nevertheless, the original method of escape from an ailing aircraft was for a flight-crew member to bail out and use a parachute to lower safely to the ground. In 1912, near Paris in Issy-Moulineaux, France, Baron d'Odkolek demonstrated an ejection system that included a canon-launched parachute with a rudimentary skirt spreader. The first known lifesaving parachute jump from a disabled airplane was not until 1916. However, it took another 53 years for this device to be incorporated into and become a critical component in the operation of zero altitude/zero velocity ejection seats.

While today's aircraft escape systems are much more sophisticated than the early methods, the parachute continues to be an integral part of a successful escape. Every one of today's most modern aircraft escape systems is built around the parachute, as the following history details.

Chapter One

PARACHUTES

While it is believed that the Chinese were making exhibition parachutes as early as 1100, the first recorded use of a parachute was circa 1600. This parachute had a wooden frame covered with canvas, and Fausto Veranzio used it to make a jump from a structure in Venice, Italy. Exhibitionists, using similarly primitive parachutes, jumped from towers for notoriety, fame, and money. As time went by, hot air balloons became the exhibitionists' standard jumping platforms.

The parachutes of then were not the parachutes we think of today. In most cases, the apex of the chute was tied to the tower or balloon with the canopy rolled or folded and rigging lines hanging down. The weight of the jumper unfolded the canopy, and the breakcord attachment holding the canopy snapped, which allowed the jumper to descend. Some of these early parachutes were not even equipped with a harness: the jumper merely hung onto the suspension lines as he jumped.

Georgia Ann "Tiny" Thompson, the first known female parachute jumper, wears the Patent Safety Pack Vest, or CoatPack, developed by her stepfather, Charles Broadwick. Before she retired in 1922, Tiny made more than 1,000 parachute jumps. *National Air and Space Museum, Smithsonian Institution (SI Neg. No. 78-1321)*

Some of these showmen even had a trapeze attached to the rigging and demonstrated their acrobatic abilities while dropping from the sky.

With the growing popularity of parachute exhibitions, the sport developed some well-known characters and favorite crowd pleasers. One well-known jumper was a diminutive girl named Georgia Ann Thompson, who stood only 4 feet, 8 inches tall and weighed 80 pounds. Not surprisingly, she was nicknamed Tiny. In 1908, at the age of 15, Tiny made her first parachute jump—from a hot air balloon owned by her stepfather, Charles Broadwick. Tiny was the first woman to make a parachute jump.

On June 21, 1913, Tiny made her first parachute jump from an airplane, over what is now known as Griffith Park, in Los Angeles. The pilot was Glenn L. Martin, who later became the head of a large aircraft manufacturing company. Tiny and Martin became a team that dazzled crowds as they toured the United States.

The parachute Tiny used was called the Patent Safety Pack Vest, or CoatPack, developed by Charles Broadwick. Before Tiny retired in 1922, she had made over 1,000 parachute jumps.

Entertaining as these exhibitions were, so many jumpers were either hurt or killed by these demonstrations that public interest waned. Nevertheless, the functionality of the parachute was clearly evident.

Thus, the first aircraft parachute jumps were not made to escape from stricken aircraft, but by daredevils or exhibitionists at air shows. In general, these exhibitionists were not bothered by the aircraft's wing bracing wires or propellers, as the pilot took off with the jumper clinging onto one of the wing struts near the wing trailing edge. These jumps were generally made in one of two ways. When it was time to jump, the parachutist pulled the ripcord and allowed the blossoming parachute to pull him or her off the wing, essentially under a completely inflated chute. The other method was to have a static line attached between the airplane and the apex of the parachute canopy. When the jumper leaped from the plane, the static line pulled the parachute out of its pack and the canopy inflated.

Parachutes built in the early days of jumping, whether from towers, hot air balloons, or aircraft, were usually crude in concept and construction. The parachute was seen as a fairly simple device, which resulted in amateur construction without the technical background required to produce a safe device. The result was often death. The fabrics used in many early parachutes were muslin, linen, cotton, and silk, with a suspension line of rope, which was usually made of hemp. It took years to find the solutions to what was later discovered to be a very complicated device.

Eject: Parachutes, Escape Mechanisms, and the Military

Joseph Pino developed the first pilot chute in 1911, in the form of a primitive cap he wore on his head. As he jumped, the cap flew off, filling with air and pulling out the main parachute. Others tried compressed air, but it was not until steel springs were sewn into the pilot chute that it became a dependable device. The pilot chute was packed on top of the main chute in a fabric pack. When the ripcord was pulled, springs pushed the pilot chute out into the airstream, where it inflated and provided sufficient aerodynamic drag to extract the main canopy for its inflation. One of the better-known pilot chutes was the one invented by Leslie Irvin and sold by the Irving Air Chute Co. of the United States (now named Irvin Aerospace).

Contrary to many people's assumption, there was not heavy use of parachutes by military aircrews during World War I. Many observers in spotter balloons wore parachutes, but few airmen did. The macho attitudes of the fliers, their feelings of invincibility, the unreliability of parachute deployment in that period, as well as the belief of some military leaders that if aircrews were provided with parachutes they might bail out rather than face a determined enemy, all prevented the

Shown here is U.S. Army Type H-1, an over-the-side, high-altitude escape system with a seat-pack parachute. Prior to bailout, the airman removed his oxygen mask and gripped an oxygen hose with his teeth. *U.S. Air Force (USAF No. 28354 AC), via National Air and Space Museum, Smithsonian Institution*

widespread use of parachutes. However, as World War I drew to a close, more flight crews began wearing parachutes, particularly German airmen.

Soon after the close of World War I, it became compulsory for British and U.S. aircrews to wear parachutes. From around

1918 through the late 1930s, Britain, Germany, and the United States funded laboratories, scientists, and engineers to study the many aspects involved in producing a safe and reliable parachute. While Germany produced the most innovative canopy designs, Britain's laboratories did the most detailed testing. Almost all of these parachute studies were in the area of lifesaving-type parachutes. It is also believed that Russia and Japan were doing much the same type of research at the time, but their closed societies kept their research efforts cloaked.

Until this time, canopies were made from a variety of fabrics. However, laboratory and drop tests proved that silk provided the best combination of porosity and strength, plus it was lightweight and easily packed. It was also fairly impervious to the environment in which it was stored. For many years thereafter, silk became the universal parachute canopy material.

It was understood that the primary duty of the parachute was to slow a falling body. But a strong secondary purpose was to stabilize the body during descent. If a stable descent were not achieved, sometimes the canopy would "spill air" (increase the rate of descent) or even collapse, resulting in great harm or death. Unstable descents made it extremely difficult for a jumper to plan his contact with the ground and minimize injury.

Studies focused on the best canopy shape to provide a stable, controlled descent.

It was not until the invention of the auxiliary, or pilot chute, that a jumper was assured his parachute would deploy from its pack, inflate properly, and provide a safe descent canopy.

On the brink of World War II, there was great concern about the availability of silk for parachutes, so much so that Great Britain returned its studies to the use of linens and cotton,

PARACHUTES

These U.S. Navy cadets are wearing seat-pack—type parachutes. Prior to entering an aircraft, they would unhook their packs from their shoulders, which would allow the parachute to drop down on its harness and become their seat cushion. *Bob Bashaw*

while the United States relied on manmade rayon and nylon for its parachute materials.

In fact, silk never regained its prominence as the choice material for parachutes. Nylon became almost the universal parachute material of choice. Part of the reason for the switch was the tight quality control that could be maintained with manmade materials. The beauty of the many years of parachute study is that it resulted in an economical device that provides a large amount of air resistance and can be packed into a small amount of space. Lightweight, reliable, and safe—all features that appear in today's sports parachute. In addition, modern-day parachutes provide excellent glide angles and allow a trained parachutist to pick the exact spot of landing and at a fairly low descent rate.

This U.S. Air Corps pilot, seated on the wing of his P-51 Mustang, is wearing a backpack parachute. The backpack parachute became the standard for World War II air crews.
The Mighty Eighth Air Force Heritage Museum

At the outbreak of World War II, Germany's parachute development was years ahead of the rest of the world. But there were many new challenges that had to be overcome. Increased aircraft speed and altitude capability began to limit the segments of flight, or flight envelope, in which an air crewman could expect to safely bail out. Also, some aircraft were still propelled by whirling pusher-propellers. In addition, many times the effort to bail out exceeded the physical strength of the airman. Most multiplace aircraft had either side or bottom bailout provisions, or sometimes both. Depending upon the aircraft's speed, gyrations, altitude, and attitude (possibly even inverted), escape could become impossible. Even then, if the airman could exit the aircraft, he might be struck by the empennage (tail) and knocked unconscious and unable to pull the ripcord—or at a minimum, be slightly injured.

Bailout from a U.S. Army Air Corps/Boeing B-17 Flying Fortress Heavy Bomber

During World War II, U.S. Army Air Corps 1st Lt. Helmuth Fredrick Hanson was the pilot of B-17F (S/N 42-29839), of the Eighth Air Force, 510th Bomb Squadron, 351st Bomb Group, based at Polebrook, England. On August 17, 1943, their bombing mission was a roller-bearing factory in Zchweinfurt, Germany.

Hanson's aircraft had a crew of 10 and joined a huge mass of American bombers in several formations and tiers. Hanson's B-17 was in the number-three position of the second element of lead squadron of the lead group. As soon as they crossed into occupied France, fighter attacks began, primarily from Focke-Wulf Fw-190s. As they approached Germany, the attacks became more ferocious and their ship came under heavy fire, resulting in their number-two engine being knocked out. The crew was able to feather the prop, and they knew their only hope of survival was to stay with their formation. They salvoed their bomb load, but even then, with only three engines, they were losing speed, and were forced into dropping back and down through the lower bomber formations and soon were outside any protection offered by the formation.

EJECT!

Like birds of prey, German fighters swarmed about them. Then there was an explosion just behind the cockpit area, followed by a huge fire. It was around 3:00 P.M. and the B-17 was at about 26,000 feet in altitude, near Mayon, Germany. Knowing his ship was mortally wounded, Hanson told the crew to bail out. But the fire had cut off the normal escape path from the cockpit. The only possible way out of the ship for Hanson and his copilot J. Z. Comfort was through the pilot's side window. Due to the limited size of the window, this escape path didn't look too promising. Comfort was able to squeeze out the window and drop outside behind the nonrotating propeller of the number-two engine. Hanson attempted to follow, but even with his small stature he couldn't make it through with his parachute. With the flames now enveloping the cockpit, he had but one choice: take off the chute and hope he could somehow get into it outside the ship.

Hanson squeezed through, pulling his parachute behind him, and fell away into the airstream. Try as he might, he could not get into the harness and he saw the ground approaching rapidly. He made one last desperate effort to save his life and put his right arm through the harness, pulled the ripcord with his left, and with his now-free left hand held his right arm tight against his chest, hoping he could maintain this grip throughout the opening shock of the parachute inflation.

The chute opening shock was so great that it literally peeled and rolled up the skin along the right forearm. Still clinging to the chute, he saw his B-17 circling him as if it were determined to kill him. Then the ship exploded without any further harm to its injured pilot. Upon landing, Hanson was immediately surrounded by several very angry farmers with pitchforks. His injuries were so great that he didn't struggle, but the farmers were so incensed that it looked as if they would use their pitchforks to kill him. In a matter of minutes, the military arrived. Hanson was glad to be put into the hands of more seemingly reasonable people. Though he was taken prisoner, Hanson was fortunate to be quickly taken to a hospital for the medical treatment he so badly needed.

Hanson made a full recovery and later found out that the entire crew, with the exception of the upper gunner, had made

Shown here is a Boeing B-17F Flying Fortress, similar to the one flown by U.S. Army Air Corps 1st Lt. Helmuth Frederick Hanson. *Boeing*

it safely out of the aircraft. The upper gunner had been hit by gunfire and his parachute had prematurely opened, within the turret, and ignited. Perhaps an oxygen bottle near the upper gunner's station was hit and ruptured by gunfire, causing the explosion and resulting intense fire.

Hanson, who spoke fluent German, was taken by train to a stalag near Frankfurt, and was able to use his language skills to escape and make his way through German lines and regain his freedom.

EJECT!

Bailout from a Martin B-26 Maurader Medium Bomber

It was World War II, and on August 18, 1944, U.S. Army Air Corps S.Sgt. Lewellyn "Lew" Case and his crewmates of the Ninth Air Force 386th Bomb Squadron were based in Chelmsford, England. They had completed 25 missions and were due for a flak leave in Scotland. This was soon after D-Day and the Allies in France had moved out of the beach-heads, but the battles were surging back and forth with no clear victory in sight. Their B-26 pilot, Lt. Malcolm McDonald, was asked to take his crew on one special mission before taking their leave. They agreed, but their Martin B-26B had already been assigned to another crew. Thus, McDonald and his five-man crew were assigned a new model, a B-26G1 (S/N 43-34211), with their primary target being a troop and tank emplacement. At the last minute they were directed to their secondary target, the marshaling yards at Orleans, France.

It was a little after noon as they approached the marshaling yards at about 8,000 to 10,000 feet in altitude, and they could see the flak building up ahead. Then, without warning, a huge flak burst caught them, immediately knocking out their right engine. They could hear flak shrapnel crashing about inside the ship, with Case feeling a thump as flak hit his seat pan. With the engine out, they knew they couldn't finish the bomb run and the bombardier, 1st Lt. Donald Van Horn, was ordered to salvo the eight 500-pound bombs. Remembering the drill, McDonald slowly increased the power of the left engine to full throttle, trimmed out the ship, and started a gentle turn to the left—away from the failed engine. Their hope, at this point, was to reach the French coastline.

Then the crew received some more bad news. Van Horn reported he could not drop the bombs either electrically or manually. The flak shrapnel had apparently cut some of the ship's wiring and manual cables. The situation was desperate, as they were losing altitude fast. Van Horn suggested that maybe with the landing gear down he could reach into the nose gear bay (the normal entry to the aircraft) to pull the severed manual-release cable and get rid of the 4,000-pound bomb load. The copilot, 1st Lt. Joseph Hauser, lowered the landing gear and the bombardier raised and latched the inner hatch open, but as the "G" was a new ship to them, they could not locate the cable.

Flight engineer/gunner S.Sgt. Walter Lile and armorer/gunner S.Sgt. Jack Carroll went into the bomb bay and were able to manually get rid of three bombs. They were still losing altitude—with 2,500 pounds of bombs remaining. It was obvious they couldn't fly any further. McDonald ordered the crew to bail out, holding the ship steady. A few seconds later, McDonald ordered Hauser to bail out as well. Case clipped on his chest pack chute, stepped into the open nose gear hatch, where he dropped out and immediately pulled his ripcord—about 600 feet above the ground.

Looking up, he saw daylight through holes in the canopy, which had been pierced in several places by the earlier flak shrapnel. Then other, mysterious holes began to appear. Case knew he was under fire from below. He landed hard in a railroad cut, crashing his face hard against a brick retaining wall. As he attempted to run, pain radiated in his ankle—later he discovered it was fractured. He attempted to pull out his .45-caliber handgun as he limped forward.

But directly ahead was a soldier, holding a rifle with a fixed bayonet. Case stopped, but the soldier didn't. He was determined to take out this American on the end of his bayonet. Just as Case thought his life was over, a German officer on top of a nearby bridge yelled for the soldier to stop. The soldier obeyed, but his momentum carried him too far. The bayonet snagged and tore Case's uniform.

Case was loaded into a motorcycle sidecar and hustled off to be interrogated: first a beating, followed by a "friendly" glass of Scotch. When the German officer realized he was only going to get Case's name, rank, and serial number, he terminated the interrogation. It was some time before Case received the medical attention he badly needed.

Case later discovered that two of their crew made it to friendly lines, just after landing. While in a German prison camp, he met Hauser and Lile, both of whom had safely parachuted out of the B-26 and were also taken prisoner. McDonald didn't have time to bail out and died in the crash. Both Van Horn and Carroll were able to evade capture and made it back to friendly lines.

Shown here is a Glenn L. Martin Company B-26 Maurader medium bomber, similar to the aircraft from which S.Sgt. Lewellyn Case was forced to bail out. *Glenn L. Martin photo, via Lockheed Martin*

Chapter Two

BASIC
EJECTION SEATS

T he ejection seat has been around since 1910, when a professor demonstrated a cartridge-and-bungee-powered
ejector seat. In 1916, George Prensiel experimented
with a compressed-air ejector seat. In 1923, E. Scheemacker
demonstrated his Concertina EjectaSeat. In 1930, the Dudgeon
Spring Load Seat made its debut. Worldwide, ejection seats
and systems have constantly been developed and improved
over the years.

German and Swedish Seats

Germany was the first country to make a determined effort
to solve the problem of getting a pilot safely out of a high-performance aircraft under conditions where the aircraft was out
of control, or in unusual attitudes of flight. Within this same
period of time, Sweden was pursuing similar studies.

Heinkel He-280V-1 Fighter

One of Germany's early jet aircraft was the single-place, twin-engine, low-wing Heinkel He-280V-1 fighter. The ship was ready for flight tests prior to the availability of its Heinkel He–S-8B turbojet engine. To obtain some preliminary flight characteristics of the aircraft, the engine nacelles were modified into streamlined pods to minimize aerodynamic drag, while still maintaining the aircraft's center of gravity, without its engines. On September 22, 1940, He-280V-1 was towed into the air by a Heinkel He-111B bomber. On this nonpowered flight, the ship was piloted by Flugbaumeister Paul Bader from the Rechlin, Germany, experimental establishment. Bader reached an altitude of 13,222 feet and a maximum speed of 174 miles per hour. Still without its turbojet engines, Heinkel wanted to further expand the envelope of this ship's flight characteristics. For this reason, at least 45 additional towed flights took place.

Heinkel recognized that higher performance required a better means of safely escaping from a disabled aircraft than over-the-side bailouts. Their solution was the one we are all familiar with today: the ejection seat.

The Heinkel ejectorseat was a development parallel with the He-280V-1s, with both beginning in late 1939. The ejector seat was tested with sandbags and anthropomorphic dummies in a ground rig at Heinkel's plant in Rechlin, Germany. Then, in a planned test, the first actual use of the Heinkel ejector seat took place from an aircraft by a trained parachutist and German military pilot named Busch.

Since it was the world's first ejection system, it is not a surprise that the seat's design and operation were quite rudimentary. But the surprise lies in the method of powering this seat. It was not powered by an explosive cartridge device, but by compressed air. This system was able to propel the 265-pound seat with a pilot weighing 176 pounds almost 19 feet above the aircraft.

BASIC EJECTION SEATS

The design, of course, was continually improved. Significant improvements began in 1943 at Heinkel's Rostock facility with the addition of an inclined ejection test ramp. Data obtained from simulated ejections using this ramp were combined with the tolerance of the human body to obtain acceptable acceleration rates. Wanting to get greater heights from the ejection seat, the air pressure in the system's storage bottle was increased in increments. As the pressure increased, the volunteers began to complain of chest and back pains. It was quickly discovered that it was not the g-forces (acceleration), but the rate of rise of acceleration that was critical.

In Germany, Dornier and Focke-Wulf, and in Sweden, Saab, were also developing ejection seats for their aircraft. All three companies began by using compressed air, but eventually switched to the use of an explosive cartridge to power their ejection seats. By late 1942, all new German designs for high-speed fighters and fighter-bomber aircraft were fitted with ejection seats. In Sweden, Saab installed an ejection seat in its J-21 fighter, which was first flown on July 30, 1943, from Linkoping, Sweden. It is believed that Saab's ejection seats, used during World War II, paralleled those of German design.

During the later stages of World War II, the change from compressed air to explosive cartridges took place in all German aircraft, although at least 60 Luftwaffe airmen owed their lives to Heinkel's original compressed-air ejection system. While the close of the war ended Germany's ejection seat production, Sweden's designs continued.

Compared to Germany and Sweden, other companies and countries were much slower to begin their study and implementation of ejection seats on their designs. Swedish ejection seat designs continued to provide the escape systems used in their military aircraft until the JAS39 Gripen, which used a Martin-Baker seat.

EJECT!

The First Emergency Ejection Using the Heinkel Compressed-Air Seat

It was decided to use the He-280V-1 (still waiting for its turbojet engines) as a flying test bed for Argus As-014 pulse jet engines—engines that were designed to power the Fiesler Fi-103 V-1 Buzz Bomb. The He-280V-1 was fitted with four of these Argus engines, but they provided insufficient power to get the aircraft into the air. With its Argus engines operating, the He-280V-1 was towed by an He-111 tug into the air from a snowy runway in icy conditions. The He-280 pilot for this early 1940s flight was Schenk. After being towed to 7,875 feet in altitude, he found that ice had frozen his towrope release mechanism. He wagged his wings to alert the tow plane to his problem, but this signal was misinterpreted as a request to release their end of the towline. Schenk was left flying an underpowered aircraft with a long towrope dangling from his aircraft's nose.

A Heinkel He-280V, the first aircraft model fitted with an ejection seat, sits aside an icy runway it slid from during a landing rollout. *National Air and Space Museum, Smithsonian Institution (SI Neg. No. 78-1321)*

Landing under such circumstances was too risky, Schenk decided, so he decided to bail out by using his ejection seat. Schenk thus became the world's first person to be saved by the use of an ejection seat. He described the event as follows: "I jettisoned the canopy and then pulled the release lever for the seat and was thrown clear of the aircraft without coming in contact with it. During the acceleration I did not lose consciousness or notice any disagreeable feeling. I realized I was revolving considerably and believe I executed a backward somersault, as I recall seeing the aircraft again. After a short time, I succeeded in jettisoning the catapult seat, which quickly fell away from me. I then pulled my ripcord and the parachute opened perfectly. The opening shock appeared more violent than that experienced during catapulting."

The He-280V-1 was destroyed in the ensuing crash, and it was another prototype that made the first flight powered by a pair of Heinkel He-S-8B turbojet engines.

While other countries were behind Sweden and Germany in developing ejection seats, Allied forces, including the British, were gathering vast amounts of advanced data and hardware from Germany even before the close of World War II. In fact, sometime in 1943, the U.S. Army Air Corps in Wright Field, Ohio, had an actual captured Heinkel ejector seat to work with.

British Seats

It was not until 1944 that the British Ministry of Aircraft Production asked James Martin of the Martin-Baker Co. to investigate the practicability of a means to assist a fighter pilot in escaping from a disabled craft. After looking at a number of methods, Martin settled on the idea of an ejection seat. The question, though, was why Martin didn't use the German test data and actual captured ejection seats as a starting point. Either the British Ministry of Aircraft Production kept this information from Martin or he chose to ignore the studies already completed in Germany, perhaps to make an independent scientific approach to solve this important problem. Whatever the reason, it slowed the development of ejection seats in Britain and throughout Europe as Martin covered much of the same ground that Heinkel had about five years earlier. In fact, even though Martin started several years ahead of other advanced aircraft in Britain, the United States, and Russia, these country's aircraft were equipped with ejection seats at about the same time as the British aircraft were.

As had been determined by German engineers and scientists, Martin found that the g-forces necessary to propel the pilot clear of his aircraft wasn't the most important element. It was the rate of rise of g-forces that was of prime concern. Obviously, to be operationally functional, the ejection process shouldn't harm its occupant. The limitation then was the acceleration forces that the human spine could withstand without damage. Seeking scientific answers, Martin actually watched spinal surgery taking place and obtained a human spine for study.

A part of Martin's answer to spinal damage was the use of the face screen as the ejection initiator. The screen would assist the pilot in having his spine in the optimum position to accept the upward acceleration required for ejection. The face screen also helped to protect the pilot's face from the windblast and would keep his helmet and oxygen mask in place. The development of Martin-Baker ejection seats continued through a series of ground and airborne ejection tests, the final result being the manual Mark 1. The Mark 1 ejection seat was tested by Martin-Baker's Bernard "Benny" Lynch as the test subject.

In June 1947, the Air Ministry chose the Martin-Baker Mark 1 for installation in the Gloster Meteor fighter, the Supermarine fighter-bomber Attacker, the Westland Wyvern, Navy strike aircraft, the English Electric Canberra bomber, and, later, the Hawker Sea Hawk and de Havilland Venom fighter-bomber aircraft.

Let's look at how the first production Martin-Baker ejection seat, Mark 1, operated. As the Mark 1 was a manual ejection system, the first step in escape was to release the canopy and

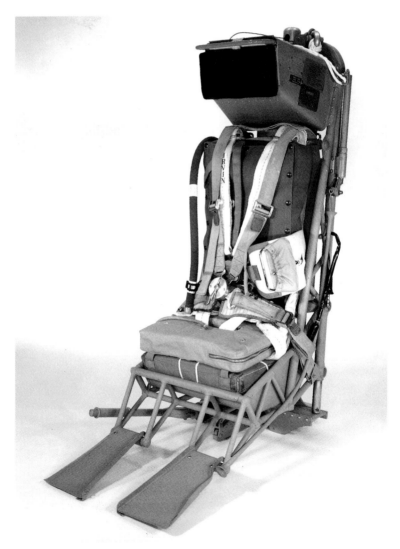

Shown here is the prototype of the Martin-Baker Mark 1 ejection seat. *Martin-Baker*

then pull down the face screen to initiate the actual ejection process. The seat was powered by an explosive-type cartridge; to minimize the rate of rise of g-forces, two lower-powered cartridges were used in a series. Upon pulling the face screen, the first cartridge fired, with the second cartridge firing moments later when it was uncovered by a moving piston. As the seat cleared the aircraft, a static line attached to the aircraft fired a drogue gun, deploying a 2-foot-diameter drogue, which stabilized the airman and seat. At that point, the airman released his seat harness, pushed himself away from the seat, and manually deployed his parachute.

While these manual ejection seats developed by Germany, Sweden, and Britain were crude by today's standards, they established the design baseline. It was upon these fundamentals that more efficient ejection seats were to follow.

The Gloster Meteor fighter was the first British production aircraft fitted with an ejection seat. Martin-Baker built the ejection seat. *National Air and Space Museum, Smithsonian Institution (SI Neg. No. 78-1321)*

Chapter Three

EARLY U.S. MANUAL EJECTION SEATS

The U.S. Navy was closely following the efforts of the Martin-Baker Co. In October 1945, Commander J. J. Ide and Lt. R. B. Barnes were impressed by the efforts being made in England and the use of the rig to test ejection seats in the laboratory. Through Ide and Barnes' efforts, the Navy approved the installation of a similar ground test rig at the U.S. Naval Yard in Philadelphia. The erection of this test rig, patterned after the British model, took place in the summer of 1946. This close working relationship between the Martin-Baker Co. and the Navy continued, and the majority of the Naval aircraft built after this time were equipped with Martin-Baker ejection seats.

When Germany surrendered, the Allies, led by the United States, literally swarmed across Europe on a project named "Operation Lusty." This code-name was for a large task force, which consisted of a variety of different technology-exploitation groups. The groups went into former combat zones immediately after hostilities ceased in order to learn of German technologies. German scientists were interviewed, files were microfilmed, and hardware was taken. U.S. Army Air Corps Col. Hal Watson also led a group of pilots who evaluated and "liberated" a wide variety of German airplanes. Naturally, the hardware and data were taken, as were the ejection seats. The technology discovered from this operation jump-started the United States' development of ejection seats.

The Wright Air Development Center in Wright Field, Ohio, was also aware of the efforts of the Martin-Baker Co. and that of the Germans, but chose a different path from that of the Navy. Essentially, the Wright Air Development Center (WADC) stepped out of the way and allowed each American aircraft manufacturer—or those whose company wished to specialize in ejection seat design—to proceed with their own escape system approach.

At the same time, the Russians were performing similar operations. Thus the Navy, the British, and many in Europe were awaiting the results from James Martin's studies in the ejection seat field. But many American and Russian aircraft companies picked up where the Germans left off and began producing their own ejection seats. Just as the German seats of this time period were of a manual type, so, too, were these American and Russian ejection seats. Some of the first American ejection seat manufacturers and the aircraft in which these seats were first installed follow.

Bell Aircraft X-1A and X-1B Research Aircraft

None of the original Bell X-1 series of research aircraft was equipped with ejection seats, and all utilized side entry doors. But with the aircraft's wing just a few feet aft of and almost centered on the door, it wouldn't have been an appealing over-the-side bailout approach. After the loss of the Bell X-1D, it was decided that ejection seats should be retrofitted. Ships X-1A and X-1B were sent back to the factory to have Bell ejection seats added. After returning to flight status, ship X-1A was lost in an in-flight explosion. This heightened the awareness of the danger involved with operating these rocket-powered ships, and the X-1B was thoroughly evaluated for its ability to operate as safely as possible.

When the dangers associated with rocket-powered aircraft were discovered, the Bell Aircraft X-1A (pictured) and X-1B rocket research aircraft were retrofitted with an ejection seat. *Bell Aircraft*

During the X-1B's evaluation, it was discovered that an error had been made in the relationship between its ejection seat and its instrument panel. If ejection had been attempted, the forepart of the pilot's feet would have been trapped beneath the instrument panel, guaranteeing serious injury.

The X-1B was past its prime and it wasn't cost effective to correct the deficiency; the ship was retired. This aircraft, the Bell X-1B (S/N 48-1385), is on display at The Air Force Museum in Dayton, Ohio. As a side note, ship X-1C was never completed, and later one of the original X-1 series was modified to utilize turbo pumps. After this modification, it was reidentified as the X-1C and is mounted on a plinth where it is displayed at Edwards Air Force Base in California.

Shown here is a rudimentary Bell Aircraft ejection seat, which was retrofitted into the X-1A and X-1B rocket research aircraft. *Bell Aircraft*

Boeing Airplane Company B-47 Stratojet Bomber

The XB-47 (S/N 46-65) was a three-place, six-engine bomber, first flown on December 17, 1947. The pilot was Robert Robbins, with Scott Osler as copilot. The flight was made from Boeing Field in Seattle.

In early-production aircraft, only the pilot and copilot were equipped with ejection seats. The B-47 had remote-controlled tail guns, which were operated by the copilot. To operate his machine guns, the copilot was required to rotate his ejection seat 180 degrees in order to face aft, allowing him to look into his cathode-ray tube radar display and operate his guns. The ejection seat was mounted on three bearings, which rode on a circular track. If ejection were required, the seat had to be in its forward-facing position.

The Boeing B-47 Stratojet was a three-place bomber, originally built with ejection seats for both the pilot and copilot. *Boeing Historical Archives*

The bombardier/navigator had to use the typical World War II over-the-side bailout technique for in-flight escape. Both Republic and Weber Aircraft provided ejection seats for these aircraft.

Shown here is the Boeing B-47 Stratojet ejection seat for the copilot, which rotated 180 degrees to enable the copilot to operate the aircraft's tail guns. *Weber Aircraft*

Chance Vought XF7U-1 Cutlass Fighter

The XF7U-1 (BuAer 122472) Cutlass was first flown on September 29, 1948, from Patuxent Naval Air Station, in Patuxent, Maryland. The pilot was Robert Baker, and the Cutlass was equipped with a Chance Vought ejection seat.

Convair XP-81 Fighter

The Convair XP-81 (S/N 44-91000) experimental long-range escort fighter was first flown on February 7, 1945, from

Muroc Army Air Field in Muroc, California. The pilot was Frank W. Davis. Only two ships were built and each was equipped with ejection seats. The seats are thought to be designed and built by Convair.

Curtiss XP-87 Blackhawk Fighter

The Curtiss XP-87, Model No. 29A, Blackhawk (S/N 45-59600), an experimental, two-place, all-weather, night fighter-interceptor was first flown on March 5, 1948, from Muroc Army Air Field in Muroc, California. Piloted by Lee Miller on its maiden flight, the experimental fighter was the only one of its kind built. It is thought that this aircraft was equipped with a Curtiss-designed-and-built ejection seat.

Douglas Aircraft Co. XA2D-1 Skyshark Fighter

The XA2D-1 (BuAer 122988) Skyshark was the first Douglas aircraft to be equipped with an ejection seat and was first flown on May 26, 1950. George Jensen made the flight from Edwards Air Force Base in California. The ejection seat designed by Douglas for this aircraft was based partially upon German data and data provided by the U.S. Navy's Air Crew Equipment Laboratory in Philadelphia.

Glenn L. Martin Co. XB-51 Bomber

The first Martin aircraft equipped with ejection seats was their Model No. 234, XB-51 (S/N 46-685) bomber. The ship was first flown on October 28, 1949, from the Martin Middle River Plant, near Baltimore, Maryland. This was a two-place, three-engine, midwing bomber of which two were built, both equipped with Glenn L. Martin ejection seats.

Grumman Aircraft XF9F-2 Panther Fighter

The first flight of this Grumman Model G-79 fighter took place on November 24, 1947, from Long Island, New York.

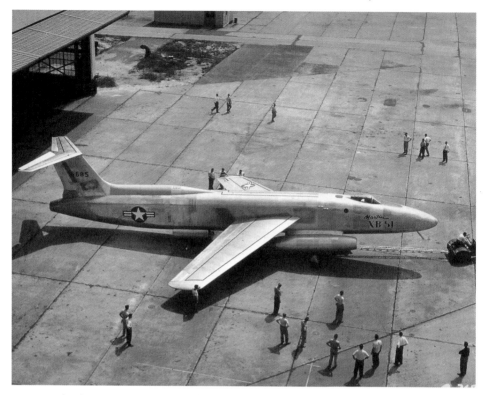

The Glenn L. Martin XB-51 was the first Martin Aircraft equipped with ejection seats.
Lockheed Martin Skunk Works

The pilot was Corwin H. Meyer, and the plane utilized a Grum-man-built ejection seat.

Lockheed P-8oC Shooting Star Fighter

The first Lockheed aircraft to be equipped with an ejection seat was the P-80C. The P-80/F-80 models prior to the P-80C were designed for over-the-side bailout, which was typical at that time. The P-80C had a manual ejection seat propelled by a cartridge. It was up to the pilot to jettison his canopy and, after ejection, release himself from the ejection seat and pull his D-ring, as he would have done in an over-the-side bailout.

The original models of the Lockheed Aircraft P-80/F-80 were not equipped with ejection seats. The F-80C was the first Lockheed model to be equipped with one and used a Lockheed-designed seat. *Lockheed Martin Skunk Works*

In addition to ground tests, Lockheed performed a number of airborne ejection tests from the rear seat of a two-place Lockheed T-33 Silverstar trainer, near the coast of the Pacific Ocean. These tests were made utilizing anthropomorphic dummies.

North American Aviation XB-45 Tornado Bomber

The first North American Aviation (NAA) aircraft to be equipped with an ejection seat was the XB-45 Tornado bomber. The first flight of the NAA Model No. NA-130 XB-45

(S/N 45-59479) was made on March 17, 1947, from Muroc Army Air Field in Muroc, California. The pilot was George Krebs, with Paul Brewer as the flight-test engineer.

Ejection seats were only provided for the pilot and copilot, with the bombardier/navigator and tail gunner utilizing typical over-the-side bailout techniques. The ejection seats were completely manual, with manual canopy jettison and an explosive cartridge firing the ejection seats. After ejection, each crew member manually released himself from the seat and pulled his parachute's D-ring.

Northrop Aircraft Corp. XP-89 Scorpion Fighter

The XP-89 Scorpion's (S/N 46-525) maiden voyage took place on August 16, 1948, from Muroc Army Air Base in Muroc, California, piloted by Charles Fred Bretcher. This fighter-interceptor was fitted with a Northrop-designed-and-built basic manual ejection seat.

Republic XF-91 Thunderceptor Fighter

This single-place, low-wing rocket and turbojet-powered fighter (S/N 46-688) was first flown on May 9, 1949, from Muroc Army Air Base in Muroc, California, by Carl Bellinger. Only two Thunderceptors were built, with the ejection seats built by Republic.

Chapter Four

UNUSUAL
ESCAPE
METHODS

Several approaches other than the use of ejection seats were tried to assist flight crews in bailing out, including propeller removers, escape slides, and escape baffles or airstream deflectors.

Propeller Removers

In the very early days of powered aircraft, pusher-propellers made safe escape from an ailing aircraft extremely difficult. As aircraft design matured, pusher-propeller designs still appeared from time to time. Propeller removers were one method used to provide safe escape prior to ejection seats.

U.S. Army Air Corps/BELL XFM-1 Airacuda
Fighter-Interceptor

The Bell XFM-1 Airacuda was a very unusual multiplace interceptor-fighter. It had a crew of five, twin-pusher engines, and was of a midwing design. The first flight of the XFM-1 (S/N 37-351) took place on September 1, 1937, from Buffalo Airport in Buffalo, New York. The pilot was U.S. Army Air Corps Lt. Benjamin S. Kelsey. A gunner's location was in the leading edge of each engine pod. These gunners normally sat in the fuselage for takeoff and landings, with access to their gunner position through a crawlway within the wing. In the event of an imminent escape while they were in their gunner's position, an explosive charge was located around the propeller shaft. This could be detonated to cut the propeller shaft, freeing the propeller and allowing over-the-side bailout for each gunner. However, it is doubtful the planned propeller remover detonators were ever installed, as only a total of 13 XFM-1 and YFM-1 Airacudas were built, with the ship never entering production.

Shown here is a Bell Aircraft YFM-1 Airacuda multiplace fighter, with gunner positions in the glassed-in leading edge of each engine nacelle. In the event of a bailout, the gunners would activate the propeller remover and bail out directly from the nacelle. *Bell Aircraft*

U.S. Army Air Corps/Curtiss XP-55 Ascender

A contender for the same contract as Vultee with its XP-54 Swoose Goose, and Northrop with its XP-56 Black Bullet, was Curtiss with its XP-55 Ascender fighter. The XP-55 had a rear-mounted engine, which drove pusher-propellers. The first flight of the three ships built (S/N 42-78845, C/N 21, and Model 24), took place on July 10, 1943, from Scott Field, near St. Louis, Missouri, piloted by Harvey Gray. The bailout scheme for the XP-55 was quite simple: an explosive charge was located around its propeller shaft. If the pilot were to bail out, a cockpit switch would sever the shaft, eliminating the propeller. As was then typical, the pilot would roll the ship over on its back and drop out of the cockpit and manually open his parachute, via the D-ring.

The Curtiss XP-55 Ascender was a rear-engine fighter. In the event of in-flight escape, the pilot would detonate an explosive charge that would sever the propeller from the aircraft. *Jim Tuttle*

The flight characteristics of the Ascender were so poor that the ship's nickname was modified to become "Ass-ender." On November 15, 1943, test pilot Harvey Gray was conducting a series of stall tests when the XP-55 suddenly flipped forward

180 degrees, onto its back, and headed toward the ground. Gray was lucky to bail out safely, never cutting loose the propellers, while the XP-55 plowed into the ground.

U.S. Army Air Corps/Northrop XP-56 Black Bullet Fighter

The XP-56 was a flying-wing fighter design and, as in the case of the XP-55, the XP-56 had an aft-mounted engine. Its propellers were a pusher type, directly behind the pilot, which made escape difficult. The first of the two XP-56s built (S/N 41-786) made its maiden flight on September 30, 1943, from Muroc Air Force Base in California and was piloted by John Meyers. The Black Bullet could never be considered a success. As in the case of the XP-55, the XP-56 also used an explosive charge mounted around its propeller shaft. This allowed the pilot, via a cockpit switch, to sever the propellers and provide

The Northrop XP-56 Black Bullet was equipped with a rear engine, which drove the pusher-propellers. An explosive charge would remove the propellers to allow an over-the-side bailout. *Northrop*

a safe path to manually bail out over the side. Although no pilot was ever forced to bail out of the ship, John Meyers had his back broken during a high-speed taxi. A vicious nose-wheel shimmy developed, flipping the ship onto its back and throwing Meyers out of the ship.

Author's Note

In my opinion, it is unlikely that the use of explosive removers was any more than a design concept for the above nonproduction aircraft. Further, detailed testing would probably have revealed that, after cutting loose these forward-thrusting propellers, their direction of travel would have been unpredictable. These large, heavy, flailing pieces of metal probably would have been as perilous to a pilot as attempting an over-the-side bailout with the propellers still in place.

Escape Slides

In the early postwar years, the U.S. Navy wasn't sure that ejection seats were warranted, given their weight and complexity. In place of ejection seats, escape slides were incorporated within the aircraft's structural design.

U.S. Navy/Douglas XF3D-1 (F-10B) Skyknight Night-Fighter

The Skyknight was a two-place, midwing, twin-turbojet designed as a night-fighter. The first flight of the Douglas XF3D-1 Skyknight (BuAer 121457) took place from Muroc Air Force Base in California on March 23, 1948, with pilot Russell Thaw. The Skyknight had an unusual escape system. In this time period, the U.S. Navy thought that ejection seats were too costly and unreliable, so the Douglas design team adopted a solution whereby the crew exited the aircraft down a chute angled 40 degrees down and aft, and running between the engine bays. Each crew seat pivoted to rotate inboard, and during an emergency escape the occupant grabbed a handrail on the rear cockpit bulkhead and launched himself feet first through a door and down the chute. Another door at the bottom of the chute was activated by an explosive release and opened forward to form a windbreak, allowing the man's body to clear the underside of the aircraft. Naturally, this type of exit required the aircraft to be essentially right side up and in somewhat level flight.

The Douglas Aircraft F3D-1 Skynight was a twin-engine night-fighter equipped with an emergency escape slide. The slide carried the crewmen between the jet engines and out the bottom of the aircraft. *Boeing Historical Archives*

While the U.S. Navy approved the escape slide, they insisted that Douglas prove it in actual flight. This was done on a series of tests carried out by a team of parachutists led by U.S. Navy Lieutenant A. J. Furtek. These test were performed from a Skyknight, where the parachutists performed in-flight escapes over a range of speeds from 139 to 444 miles per hour, all of which were successful. The test also included several escapes

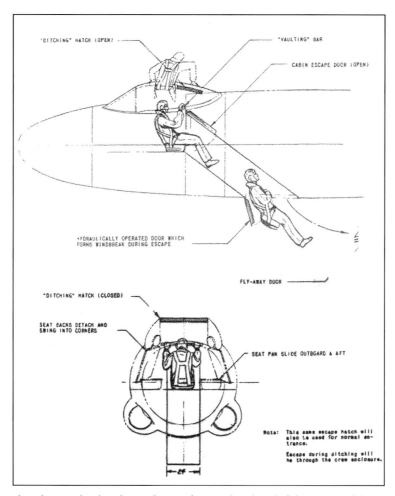

These drawings show how the Douglas Aircraft F3D-1 Skyknight night-fighter's escape slide system operated. *Douglas Aircraft*

EJECT!

made while the aircraft was in high-g-force turns to see if the crewmen could leave the aircraft under these conditions. For higher speeds—up to 500 miles per hour—anthropomorphic dummies were used with equal success.

U.S. Navy/North American Aviation XA2J-1

The XA2J-1 was a three-place, twin-turboprop, high-wing attack aircraft designed for carrier operations. NAA designed the XA2J-1 to incorporate ejection seats for its crew members. XA2J-1 (BuAer 124439) was first flown on January 4, 1952, from Los Angeles Municipal Airport. The pilot was Robert Baker, assisted by C. E. Poage. Unfortunately, the problems with the complicated Allison turboprop engine doomed this to be the only ship to reach flight status, with the second ship living out its life on the ground. None entered production.

While NAA's preliminary design included the use of ejection seats, the U.S. Navy didn't feel the capability, cost, and

The North American Aviation XA2J-1, a three-place, carrier-based, turbo-prop–powered attack aircraft, formed an escape slide out the bottom of the aircraft. The crew would use a trapezelike bar to propel themselves down the slide and outside of the aircraft. *North American Aircraft*

weight increases associated with ejection seats was worth their inclusion. Thus, North American was directed to look at the escape-slide approach that Douglas Aircraft was about to include in their design proposal for its XA3D-1. As the Navy was paying for the design, North American took this suggestion as a directive. The elimination of the ejection seats and incorporation of the escape slide required a complete revision of the mold lines to the forward fuselage of the XA2J-1. Thus, the mold lines of the XA2J-1 and Douglas XA3D-1 are nearly identical.

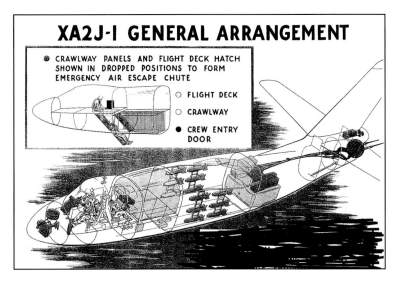

XA2J-I GENERAL ARRANGEMENT

CRAWLWAY PANELS AND FLIGHT DECK HATCH SHOWN IN DROPPED POSITIONS TO FORM EMERGENCY AIR ESCAPE CHUTE

○ FLIGHT DECK
○ CRAWLWAY
● CREW ENTRY DOOR

This drawing shows the operation of North American Aviation's XA2J-1 escape slide system. *North American Aviation, via Boeing Aerospace*

Because the XA2J-1 had a pressurized crew station, the first step in utilizing the escape slide would have required cabin depressurization. Because of the prior live and anthropomorphic dummy testing done on the Douglas Skyknight, the Navy did not require live tests of the North American escape slide. Even so, a number of ground tests were performed to validate the operation of the system, including test subjects sliding down and out onto cushions on the hanger floor. The slide was never called upon in actual flight operations.

U.S. Navy/Douglas XA3D-1 Skywarrior Attack Aircraft

The XA3D-1 Skywarrior was a three-place, twin-turbojet, high-wing attack aircraft designed for aircraft carrier operations. The Skywarrior was first flown on October 28, 1952, from Edwards Air Force Base in California, and the pilot was George Jansen. A total of 282 Skywarriors were built.

Shown here is a Douglas Aircraft XA3D-1 carrier-based attack aircraft. Note the entry ladder/emergency escape slide directly aft of the nose landing gear. *Douglas, via Boeing Historical Archives*

The Skywarrior's escape system was enhanced over that of the earlier Douglas escape-slide-equipped aircraft, the XF3D-1. On the ground, the Skywarrior was normally entered and exited through the ventral door of the emergency escape chute. Foot- and handholds were provided on the smooth surface of the chute. Together, the inner and outer escape chute doors served as an emergency exit of the aircraft whether on the ground or in flight. In an emergency, the bottom fuselage skin (the outer portion of the emergency chute) was powered through cartridge-fired cylinders and remained open up to the aircraft design limit speeds. This provided a windscreen for

Here an airman enters the cockpit area of a Douglas Aircraft A3D Skywarrior. This entry ladder was also used as the in-flight emergency escape slide. *Boeing Historical Archives*

the crew during a bailout. The inner door, which formed the floor of the cockpit, also served as a companionway for access to the bomb bay. For emergency escape, the inner door was pulled down through a mechanism tied to the lower powered door.

Prior to opening the inner door, the cabin had to be depressurized. The escape chute was completely confined with smooth walls to effect a safe exit. A sliding rectangular hatch in the canopy above and between the seats of the pilot and the navigator served as a primary escape route in the event of ditching and as an alternate bailout route. Normal procedure called for the upper hatch to be left open during takeoff and landing. Just as in the case of the XA2J-1, due to the prior live and anthropomorphic dummy testing done on the Skyknight, the U.S. Navy did not require live tests of the escape slide.

Escape Baffles or Airstream Deflectors

As aircraft speeds increased over the years, it became more difficult for an airman to push himself out into the

The AJ-1 Savage was the first North American Aviation carrier-based aircraft capable of carrying an atomic bomb. *North American Aviation, via Boeing Aerospace*

strong, turbulent airstream for a typical "over-the-side"–type bailout. For that reason, baffles, or airstream deflectors, were installed adjacent to the escape hatches to assist crew members in their exit of the aircraft.

U.S. Navy/North American Aviation XAJ-1 Savage Attack Aircraft

The XAJ-1 had a three-man crew, two reciprocating engines, and one turbojet and a high-wing design. It was the first carrier-based aircraft equipped to carry an atomic bomb.

The AJ-1 Savage relied on conventional over-the-side bailout for an in-flight escape. The forward portion of the crew entry door also served as an airstream deflector, as shown in this photo. *North American Aviation, via Boeing Aerospace*

EJECT!

The first flight of the XAJ-1 (BuAer 121460) took place from Los Angeles Municipal Airport on July 3, 1948, piloted by Robert Chilton. In addition to the three XAJ-1s, 133 AJ-1s, AJ-2s, and AJ-2Ps were built. The normal crew entry on the Savage was a door on the starboard (right) side of the crew compartment, hinged on the forward side. To bail out, the crew actuated an escape lever on the normal side entry door. Pressure from a hydraulic accumulator forced the door open, ejecting the aft 2/3 portion of the door. The forward remaining 1/3 portion of the door formed a baffle, or airflow deflector. This helped to disrupt the buffeting associated with the open door and allowed crew escape using their normal parachutes. This same technique was used on the follow-on models, AJ-2 and AJ-2P, but in order to save weight and cost the deflector was manually operated, which eliminated the hydraulic accumulator and its associated components.

Shown here is the airstream deflector used on the McDonnell Douglas C-17 Globemaster III cargo aircraft, which eased the task of paratroopers exiting the aircraft.
Boeing Historical Archives

Shown here is a McDonnell Douglas C-17 Globemaster II cargo aircraft with an airstream deflector. *Boeing Historical Archives*

U.S. Navy/Douglas TA-3B Skywarrior Attack Aircraft

The Douglas TA-3B was a later version of the Douglas XA3D-1/A3D-1 Skywarrior. The baffle on the TA-3B was much larger than that of the Savage, which made it more effective. These baffles are still being used on more modern aircraft, such as the U.S. Air Force/Douglas C-17 Globemaster III cargo aircraft, to ease the task of paratroopers exiting the aircraft.

Chapter Five

AUTOMATIC EJECTION SEATS

While manual ejection seats were certainly capable of getting the airman clear of an ailing aircraft, many times spinal injuries resulted, due to the acceleration forces imposed by these early seat catapults. In addition, many crew members were not surviving the ejection, for several reasons. Generally, most seats tumbled upon entering the airstream. Some of this tumbling was so violent that the crewman was disoriented, or so confused that he forgot to disconnect the seat harness, and the crewman would ride the seat to his death. Others remembered to disconnect their seat harness but forget to pull their parachute's ripcord. Some pulled their parachute ripcord without disconnecting their seat harness.

Another problem was that many times airmen were too low to allow time to disconnect their seat harness, push away from the seat, pull their D-ring, and get a fully inflated parachute.

High altitudes also presented problems, such as cold and a lack of oxygen. Either of these could kill the crew member or reduce his physical or mental ability to pull the D-ring at lower altitudes.

The solutions to these problems weren't clear-cut. It took a number of years to solve these problems, breaking them down one step at a time. Many decisions and inventions went into the development of improved automatic ejection seats, including the replacement of explosive cartridge–powered catapults with rocket catapults. Timers, drogue chutes, barometric release mechanisms, seat separators, and bailout oxygen bottles were some of the most significant adjustments. So let's look at early automatic ejection seats to see how the devices operated and how their qualities and components were introduced into later ejection seats. Every ejection seat depends upon the parachute for recovery, and in 1912 an invention way ahead of its time was introduced. Baron Odkolek demonstrated a parachute cartridge–fired spreader system, which is critical to the zero altitude/zero gravity ejection seat—which didn't arrive on the scene until 1965.

Martin-Baker Seats Used in U.S. Aircraft

Martin-Baker became the world's largest manufacturer of ejection seats and took the lead in introducing automatic ejection seats. The design began with locating the survival gear in the seat pan and the personal parachute in a container behind the crewman. The drogue chute provided the necessary stability of the seat in the airstream. Then, after five seconds, a clockwork mechanism transferred the aerodynamic drag provided by the drogue chute from the seat to the airman's parachute. This action released the occupant from the seat and allowed the drogue to tip him forward, while pulling the personal parachute by its apex. The ejection seat then fell away, with the occupant now descending from under his parachute.

Martin-Baker also solved the difficulties of the high-altitude ejection by installing a barostat, or barometric device. Prior to this development, if ejection took place at high altitude and was accompanied by automatic parachute deployment, there was a good chance the airman would freeze or die from lack of oxygen while slowly descending. The barostat prevented the deployment of the parachute until the occupant was at 10,000 feet in altitude. If ejection occurred at or below 10,000 feet, the barostat was not involved in parachute deployment.

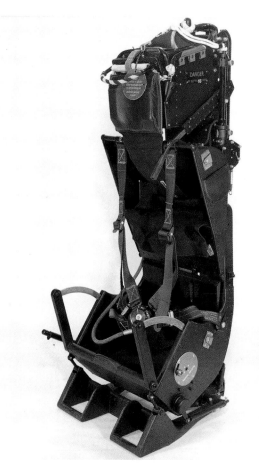

The Mark 2 ejection seat solved many of the flaws of prior ejection seats. *Martin-Baker*

These features were incorporated into the Martin-Baker Mark 2 ejection seats, along with a redesigned drogue gun. The design was such that the modifications could be retrofitted into existing Martin-Baker Mark 1 seats. This retrofitting effort began in August 1953 on ejection seats installed in a number of existing British aircraft as well as to a number of Martin-Baker seats, which were installed in U.S. Navy aircraft.

James Martin knew that aircrews would not use Martin-Baker ejection seats unless they were confident it could save their lives. Thus he hired Bernard Lynch, P. J. Page, and W. T. H. "Doddy" Hay to demonstrate the seat's ability to save lives. These men literally put their lives on the line as they rode these early seats from ground and airborne tests. In some of these tests these men suffered great injuries to their bodies—they were truly heroes who sacrificed their bodies to ensure that future aircrews could safely eject from crippled aircraft.

Although the Mark 2 ejection seat utilized an improved catapult, its explosive cartridges were still resulting in spinal injuries.

U.S. Air Force/Lockheed T-33 Silverstar Trainer

The T-33 Silverstar was a two-place, single-engine trainer. It was first flown on April 22, 1946, from Lockheed Air Terminal in Burbank, California, and was piloted by Anthony W. LeVier. The Silverstar was also purchased by the U.S. Navy as the TV-2 and 1A and sold to many foreign countries. While Lockheed built ejection seats for the Silverstar, some of those used by the U.S. Navy and Marine Corps were instead equipped with Martin-Baker ejection seats.

Ejecting from a Lockheed T-33 (TV-2) Silverstar, by Jim Boyer

It was in May 1961 and I was a 28-year-old chief warrant officer in the U.S. Marine Corps. Together with 1st Lt. John "Smokey" Calwell, we were going to U.S. Marine Corps Base in Yuma, Arizona, for the weekend, with a Monday return.

EJECT!

We took off on Saturday morning in a Lockheed T-33B. This trainer had been modified to replace its Lockheed ejection seats with Martin-Baker automatic Mark 2 ejection seats. The flight plan was easy: fly from El Toro Marine Base, California, east to the Salton Sea, and take a right to Yuma. We had just made the right turn to Yuma when the girl started to run a little rough.

We were at about 8,500 feet in altitude and at about 175 knots when the exhaust gas temperature started to peg out. Right about then we got a fire warning light and that old engine started to seize up. We were only about 10 minutes out of Marine Corps Air Station in Yuma, but with the engine beginning to seize I knew we weren't going to make it. I told

Shown here is a Lockheed T-3 Silverstar two-place trainer, which was normally equipped with a Lockheed ejection seat. In the case of Jim Boyer's bailout, the standard seat had been replaced by a Martin-Baker seat. *Lockheed*

Smokey to get ready, because we were going out. Smokey didn't like that, but it sure beat the alternative. So we started the procedure: oxygen mask on, visor down and locked, harness restraint lever to the lock position, and feet on pedals (unless you want to lose a foot, this is a must!). As I held the stick, I cranked in nose-down trim to make sure she went down hard and didn't linger topside with us. I told Smokey to hold on, and then selected command eject, which would put Smokey out first, with me following. I let go of the stick and put my hands on the face curtain.

The next sequence of events was just a blur. As I pulled the curtain, it felt like a kick in the butt with a big boot. I remember the wind on my body. When the curtain pulled away from the seat I knew that the main parachute had deployed. I looked up and that chute looked beautiful. I looked to my right and Smokey was about 20 yards away. That old Martin-Baker seat used a 24-foot flat canopy, which tends to let you down in a hurry, and looking down it looked like I was about to land in the Mexican-American Canal. Being as our flight was over land, we didn't wear flotation gear. I hit the ground, in the soft sand only about 4 feet from the edge of the canal.

We had given our position before we ejected, but even so we were stuck in what looked like a giant sandbox. It was about 45 minutes before we were picked up, and we were taken to Yuma's sick bay where the doctor looked us over and said we were fit for duty.

I didn't know it at the time, but I suffered a compression fracture of my third and fourth lumbar vertebrae. The crash investigation clearly showed that the main engine bearing had failed.

U.S. Navy/McDonnell F4H-1 Phantom II Fighter

The McDonnell F4H-1 Phantom II was a two-place fighter built for the U.S. Navy. Robert C. Little took the ship for its first flight from Lambert Field in St. Louis, Missouri, on May

27, 1958. The ship was later redesignated as the F-4 and was one of the few carrier base–designed aircraft that was later purchased by the U.S. Air Force. Some early F-4s were equipped with U.S.-built ejection seats, but most were equipped with Martin-Baker seats.

This McDonnell F-4E was the 5,000th F-4 Phantom built. Other than the crew escape module built for the F-111, McDonnell Aircraft didn't build escape systems. Martin-Baker built the F-4 fighter's ejection seats. *McDonnell Aircraft*

Ejecting from a McDonnell Aircraft F-4 Phantom, by Jim Boyer

The guys had nicknamed me "Speedy." In 1970, I was a captain with Marine Fighter/Attack Squadron 115, The Silver Eagles, out of Da Nang, Vietnam. We were flying McDonnell F-4B Phantoms, while the U.S. Air Force was flying F-4Es, but what the hell—you make do with what you've got. I'll tell you one thing: my F-4B, nicknamed Easy Rider, was the baddest cat in the alley!

AUTOMATIC EJECTION SEATS

On this mission, my radar-intercept-operator was Capt. John "Tank" Gorman. Tank had been around the block a couple of times and knew his job better than most! We had gone down to Operations to get our assignments, and we drew Hill 451 just outside An Tan. This position was close to Chu-Lai, north of Da Nang and south of Hue. The mission was to deliver close air support using Snake-Eye high-drag 250-pound bombs and napalm. The term we used to describe this type of mission was to deliver "snakes and napes."

We took off at 1300 on September 20, 1970, for the destination of An Tan Hiting. The target went smooth enough, and when we had dropped all that we came with, I should have put ol' Easy Rider's nose toward Da Nang, but not me! I just had to see what was on the other side of that hill. Well I did, and it was a $2.50-a-week Vietcong with a 37-millimeter AAA gun with our name written all over it. We took two hits in the starboard engine and it didn't seem too bad at first. I applied power and got up about 5,500 feet, and that is when I got the fire-warning light. Everything started to turn to mud about this time. You know the drill: power "off," fuel "off," fire extinguisher "on."

I applied power to the port engine but I knew she wouldn't take much more. The hydraulics were going out and we were shaking like hell wouldn't have it. I'm sure it was the compressor blades coming off. I prayed that the engine would keep spooling and not freeze up. I put her nose toward the coast, as I knew if we could get over water we would make it. I knew I was taking a chance keeping that ol' bird going but I felt if we went into the jungle we would be a guest of the Vietcong. I asked Tank and he said, "You're driving this bus, Speedy, go for it!"

We were really loping by this time and had just made the coast, but I couldn't tell how far out we were. I asked Tank what he thought and he said, "Ol' man, there's smoke coming

63

up through the floorboards. You keep talking and you and Easy Rider are going to be flying by yourselves." Our radio was out so there wasn't going to be any Mayday. I told Tank to get ready because we're getting out of here.

Once again in my career I put the Martin-Baker—this time a Mark H5 ejection system—in the "Command Eject" mode. I positioned myself, cranked in all the nose-down trim I could, and, remembering to keep my elbows tucked in, I put my hands on the face curtain and pulled down as hard as I could. The canopy went, Tank went, and I went! It felt like a giant hand of semihard air got under my butt and pushed me out and away. I felt the face curtain come loose and knew that the chute had deployed.

We entered the water with no problems. We inflated the rubber ducks, tied them together, and settled in. We would use the hand-held emergency rescue radio for a very short period, every hour on the half. At that time our survival kits had no sun hats, and the solar still, which would make drinkable water for years, was removed from the kit. It was replaced with two 12-ounce cans of water. I have often wondered who the genius was who made that decision.

On the third day, at 1615, we saw a black Lockheed C-130 not too far off. Tank and I said to hell with worrying about the Vietcong finding us and we set off smoke, flares, and starburst shells. We saw that big bird bank hard to the right. I turned on the radio and gave him a back azimuth as he closed on us. Over the radio, we heard this voice with a deep southern drawl, say, "What are you boys doing down there?" Tank jumped in and said, "We're fishing and we've had enough." About 20 minutes later here came the search-and-rescue helicopter, thanks to the ol' boy in the Herky Bird. We stabbed our rafts and sank them so they wouldn't be sucked up by the rotor blades.

Once we got onboard, I asked one of the boys if they had a smoke. Tank asked for a drink. One of the boys offered him a drink of water, and Tank said, " I've been in water for 74 hours. Don't you have anything that men drink?" We were taken to Key-Ha. That was the home of Marine Helo Unit VMO-6, code-named Barrel Hose. The flight surgeon checked us out and as far as he was concerned, with a little rest, food, and lots of liquids, we were fit for duty. The Helo Boys had a little club in a hut called "Blind Madness." We went in and the bartender asked, "What'll it be?" I told him I wanted a beer so cold that when I put it to my lips it would stick like a pump handle in December. Just having been fished out of the drink, we didn't have any money and the barkeep said with a grin: "It's on the house."

The crew of the black-painted C-130 Herky literally saved our lives—God bless them! We tried to find and thank them, but never could. We knew the black-painted C-130 wasn't one of our regular units and assumed it was with Air America, a part of the CIA secret operation. I was sent back to my beloved Marine base at El Toro, California, in September 1971. Tank stayed on for another tour. Three days before Christmas 1971, Capt. John "Tank" Gorman became one of the 58,000 men who didn't make the "Freedom Bird" back home.

Ejection Systems Used in the United States

The Martin-Baker Co. provided almost all of the ejection seats for Europe and the majority of those for the U.S. Navy. In the U.S. Air Force, it was basically left up to each aircraft manufacturer or seat manufacturer to provide the solutions needed to bail out with an automatic ejection seat.

An early automatic seat was the NAA ejection seat installed in the YF-86D Sabre. The company completely redesigned the manual ejection seat used in its earlier XB-45, B-45, and RB-45 Tornados; F-86A and E and F Sabres; and FJ-2 and FJ-3 Furys. The redesigned seat was introduced in the YF-86D Sabre, which was first flown on December 22, 1949.

EJECT!

This was an automatic ejection seat, with features similar to the automatic Martin-Baker Mark 2, but still utilizing explosive cartridges and certainly not capable of zero altitude/zero gravity performance. Even though the ejection seat in the F-86D and others of this period were automatic, they were quite limited in relation to the ejection seats later available.

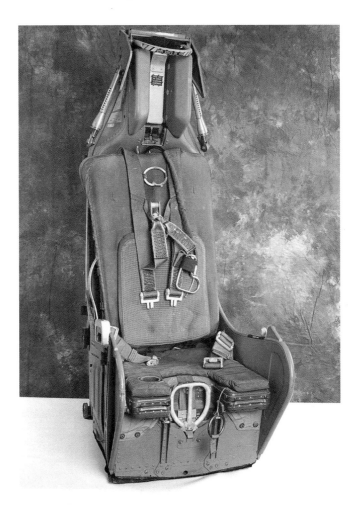

Here is a front view of a Douglas Aircraft Escapac IC-2, a zero altitude/zero gravity ejection seat used in the LTV A-7 Corsair II. It utilized an inflatable bladder, which appears as a seat cushion, to separate the pilot from the seat after ejection. *U.S. Navy*

Shown here is the ACES ejection seat built by Weber Aircraft for the General Dynamics F-16 Fighting Falcon fighter. *Weber Aircraft*

Shown here is an ACES ejection seat built by Weber Aircraft for the McDonnell Aircraft F-15 Eagle fighter. *Weber Aircraft*

AUTOMATIC EJECTION SEATS

A good example of a much-improved automatic seat was the Douglas Aircraft Escapac installed in the Ling Temco Vought A-7 Corsair II. The Corsair II XA-7 (BuAer 152580) was a single-place, twin-engine attack aircraft designed for operation aboard U.S. Navy aircraft carriers. It was taken on its

(continued on page 73)

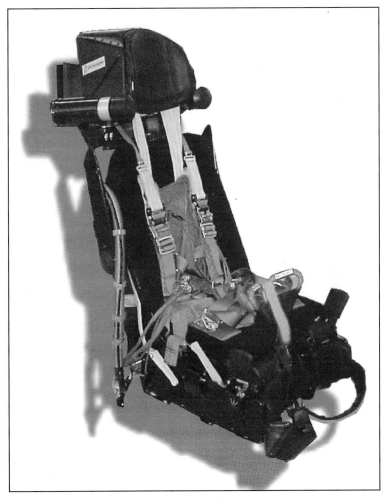

Zvezda and Goodrich Advanced Egress Systems, Inc., formerly The IBP Aerospace Group, Inc., utilized the K-36D/3.5 ejection seat design and adapted it for U.S. application. The seat shown is the K-36D/3.5. *Zvezda, via Gordon Cress*

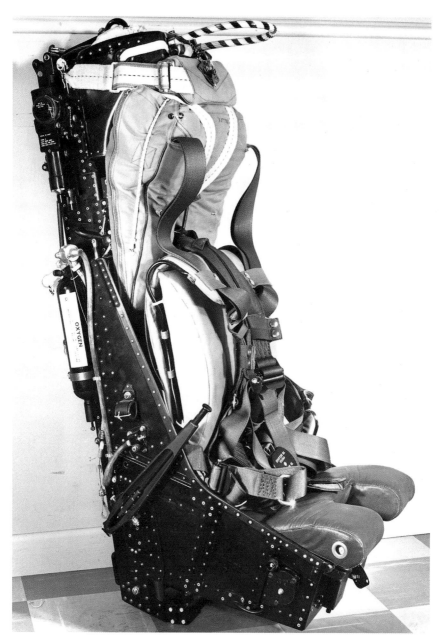

Shown here is a Martin-Baker Mark 4 fully automatic ejection seat equipped with a rocket catapult. This seat is similar to the one Jim Boyer used to eject from his F4-B Phantom. *Martin-Baker*

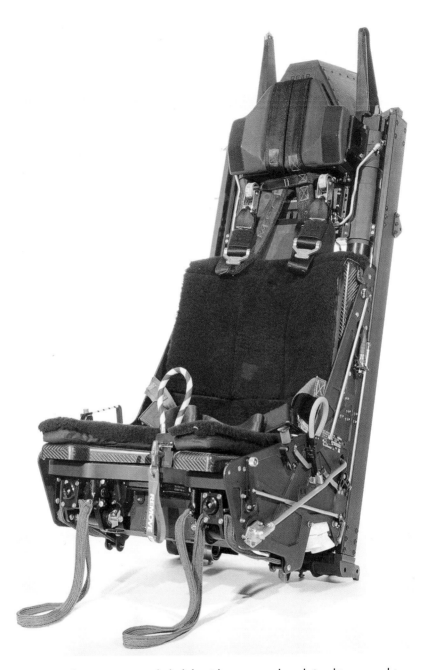

Martin-Baker 16L ejection seat had a lightweight structure and was designed to accommodate a wide range of sizes of both female and male pilots. *Martin-Baker*

Mk.16L
LIGHTWEIGHT EJECTION SEAT

Shown here in a test, the Martin-Baker Mark 16L's light weight allowed for its use in small trainer-type aircraft. The Mark 16L could accommodate a weight range of 106 to 201 pounds and a height range of 5 feet, 2 inches to 6 feet, 2 inches. *Martin-Baker*

(Continued from page 69°)

maiden flight on September 27, 1965, from the LTV plant in Dallas. The A-7A and subsequent models were equipped with a zero altitude/zero gravity seat Escapac IC-2 seat with a rocket catapult, capable of providing safe ejection operation up to 600 knots.

USSR Seats Used in the United States

Due to the closed society of the USSR, little was known in the West about their escape systems. But with the breakup of the Soviet Empire, several escape systems have become known. However, to the best of my knowledge the only one being considered for use on American aircraft is the Russian Zvezda K-36D.

The Zvezda K-36D has successfully completed qualification testing and is in service on Russian aircraft. *Zvezda*

EJECT!

The Russian Zvezda K-36D

Of the Russian ejection seats, the Zvezda K-36D is probably the best known. Several dramatic public events brought the capability of this seat to the attention of the world. The first of these events was during the 1989 Paris Air Show, where the pilot of a disabled Russian Mikoyan-Gurevich MiG-29 ejected safely, just prior to ground impact. The second event took place at the International Air Show at Fairford, England, in 1993. Here, a low-altitude midair collision took place between a pair of MiG-29s. Even though both aircraft were severely damaged, both pilots ejected safely. On June 12, 1999, at the Paris Air Show at Le Bourget Airfield, a Russian Sukhoi Su-30MKI was performing a flight demonstration. During a maneuver, the pilot pulled out of a loop too low, with the rear fuselage of the twin-engine aircraft striking the ground. This caused the left engine thrust-vectoring tailpipe to break away. The pilot initiated the aircraft's automatic ejection sequence, and at about 180 feet in altitude both crew members ejected safely.

The K-36D ejection seat used in these and other Russian aircraft, such as the Sukhoi Su-27, came from the Zvezda Research Development and Production Enterprise in Tomilino, Russia, with design efforts led by Professor Guy Severin. The results of these public ejections from Russian aircraft led to an arrangement between the United States and Russia that could not have happened just a few years earlier. Engineers and scientists from the Air Force Research Laboratory and the U.S. Navy's Air and Surface Warfare Centers were invited to visit Russian test facilities, where they witnessed a number of low- and high-altitude ejections from a modified MiG-25 aircraft and a high-speed ejection from a rocket-propelled sled. Some testing was also conducted at the sled track at Holloman Air Force Base in New

Mexico. The K-36D demonstrated safe ejections at 730 KEAS (Mach 1.25) and with a pressure suit at Mach 2.6 at 85,000 feet in altitude.

These meetings between the United States and Russia resulted in a study for a lightweight version of this 234-pound seat with a smaller headrest and the capability for a wider range of sizes and weights for its occupants. Currently, there is strong interest in producing this upgraded seat in the United States. The lightweight version would be identified as the K-36/3.5, and the limited testing done has shown its capabilities have not been degraded. A U.S.-built, 176-pound version of this seat was being studied for use on the Boeing/Lockheed Martin F-22 Raptor. The seat is also being considered for use on the U.S. Joint Strike Fighter. Goodrich Advanced Egress Systems, Inc., formerly The IBP Aerospace Group, Inc., and Zvezda are working together through a joint venture named AESI/Zvezda, Inc., to complete the adaptation and qualification of the K-36/3.5A for U.S. aircraft. Upon successful completion of qualification, AESI/Zvezda, Inc., is planning to produce and maintain the ejection seat for U.S. aircraft. An overview of the K-36 ejection seat design appears not so much a new concept, but the combination of a number of proven features seen in prior seats. These features include combined telescoping stabilization booms and parachutes (YF-107A and XB-70A), windblast deflector (X-15), and gyroscopic roll control (ACES-II).

Another interesting feature of the K-36D ejection system is that not only did Zvezda design and fabricate the ejection seat, he was also responsible for the design and fabrication of the pilot's helmet, visor, and oxygen mask. When required by the flight envelope, Zvezda also designed and built the pressure suit. To this author's knowledge, none of the other escape system manufacturers had that control or capability.

Chapter Six

INGENUITY AND VALOR:
THE PERFECT EJECTION

None of the early Martin-Baker seats, nor any of the early seats being built for the U.S. Air Force by a variety of U.S. manufacturers were anywhere near zero altitude/zero velocity in capability. Due to the type of explosive catapults being used, spinal injuries were still occurring in many cases. None of these seats could reliably provide a safe exit from a disabled aircraft that was flying too low, too high, or too fast. Injury-free ejections, within the "design-safe" ejection envelope, could not always be relied upon. Zero altitude/zero gravity, high-altitude, and high subsonic speed ejection seats had to await future developments.

Not only did it require determined scientific efforts, but also heroic actions by volunteers to finally achieve the required result: ejection seats that provide a high probably of injury-free ejection under a wide set of conditions. The stripping of the airman's helmet, visor, and oxygen masks during ejection was commonplace, as was violent tumbling upon entering the airstream. Overcoming these serious problems took a great deal of devotion on the part of engineers, scientists, doctors, and some very brave volunteers, as outlined next.

Army Air Service Capt. Hawthorne C. Gray

In the 1920s, it was well known that flights above 15,000 feet in altitude required breathing oxygen. What was not known was what type of oxygen regulators were required and what the upper limits would be in an unpressurized cockpit. Aeromedical pressure/vacuum chambers were not available, so another method had to be chosen to answer these questions. A high-altitude balloon flight, carrying an open basket, was the method used. U.S. Army Air Service Capt. Hawthorne Gray was the oxygen regulator designer and performed the actual tests from the balloon. In 1927, Hawthorne made the first test from Scott Field in Belleville, Illinois. The subfreezing temperatures at high altitude almost immobilized Gray and also froze up his oxygen system. He was forced to end the flight.

For the next test, the oxygen system was redesigned to include heaters, and Hawthorne utilized an oxygen mask rather than a hose clamped in his mouth. On this flight, he attained an altitude of 42,240 feet, but, again, the cold almost killed him. The test was repeated a third time on November 27, 1927, with improved barometric measuring devices. On this occasion, Gray reached an altitude in excess of 44,000 feet, but died in the effort. He wasn't found until the next day and was still in his balloon basket, which had landed in Sparta, Tennessee. Local doctors assumed he had either died from lack of oxygen or heart failure. His wife received the Distinguished Flying Cross posthumously for his valiant efforts. But his test was not in vain, as he had brought back proof that if a man were properly protected from the subfreezing temperatures, he could breathe at that altitude in an unpressurized environment.

Dr. Donald D. Flickinger

Dr. Donald D. Flickinger was a Stanford graduate and medical doctor who served with the U.S. Army Air Corps during World War II. A number of times he parachuted to reach crash sites in the Burma-China Hump. He provided medical aid to the survivors and assisted in the recovery of these crews.

Flickinger continued in military service after the close of the war in the area of aeromedical research at WADC. He was instrumental in getting certain survival equipment items added to procurement specifications and in the development of high-altitude ejection equipment such as bailout oxygen bottles and barometric parachute release mechanisms. Flickinger retired from the Air Force as a brigadier general. Many of the devices on which he had an impact are now standard equipment on ejection seats built around the world.

U.S. Army Air Corps 1st Sgt. Lawrence Lambert

The first airborne live ejection in the United States was made by U.S. Army Air Corps 1st Sgt. Lawrence Lambert as the test subject. This was accomplished using a U.S.-built ejection seat; the test was conducted on August 17, 1946. The standard rear seat of a Northrop P-61 Black Widow was removed and in its place an ejection seat was installed. For obvious reasons, the ship was then nicknamed "Jack-in-the-Box." The test was conducted at Wright Patterson Army Air Base in Ohio; the purpose of the test was to provide American airmen with the confidence that ejection seats could save their lives.

INGENUITY AND VALOR: THE PERFECT EJECTION

U.S. Navy Lieutenant Furtek

The U.S. Navy modified a Douglas A-26 Invader to install a Martin-Baker ejection seat in the rear gunner's position. Lieutenant Furtek volunteered to make this live demonstration, which took place on November 1, 1946. This was the first live usage of a Martin-Baker ejection seat in the United States. Just as in the case of U.S. Air Force 1st Sgt. Lawrence Lambert, this live ejection test was done to give Navy airmen confidence in the safety provided by ejection seats.

U.S. Army Air Corps Capt. Vincent Mazza

It became obvious that hearing of the success of ejection seats and actually seeing an ejection take place were two different things. For this reason, former bomber pilot U.S. Army Air Corps Capt. Vincent Mazza volunteered to take an ejection show on the road. A team was formed and, using a modified Lockheed P-80 Shooting Star, the tour group traveled to a number of Air Corps bases to demonstrate live ejections. The first of these demonstrations was conducted over San Pablo Bay in San Francisco, with Mazza ejecting from the P-80 at 10,000 feet in altitude and at 500 miles per hour.

Dr. John Paul Stapp

Dr. John P. Stapp received his master's degree in zoology and chemistry at Baylor University, his Ph.D. in biophysics from the University of Texas, and earned his medical degree at the University of Minnesota. He joined the Army Air Corps and was a witness to the first American live ejection test, which took place in August 1946 at Wright Field in Ohio. This inspired him to work in a field of study associated with escape systems and high-speed and high-altitude flight. In that field, he worked with Donald Flickinger at the WADC. Stapp volunteered to be the live subject making a high-altitude flight in an unheated and unpressurized cabin. A Boeing

B-17 was modified to reach altitudes above its normal design limit. In this grueling flight, Stapp experienced breathing oxygen at an altitude of 47,000 feet in an environment many degrees below zero. From these and similar flights, he discovered that if a person were to prebreathe 100 percent oxygen 30 minutes prior to high-altitude flight, he could avoid painful aeroembolism—when nitrogen gas bubbles form an obstruction in the blood stream (more popularly known as the bends).

Stapp talked his way into representing Wright Field as Northrop Aircraft was constructing a 2,000-foot-long, high-speed sled track at Muroc Air Force Base in Southern California's Mojave Desert. When he was unable to get Air Force funding for a crash helmet for use on the high-speed track, he talked the University of Southern California into designing one and donating it to the project. When the track became operational in the winter of 1947, he insisted on being the first live subject. By May 1948 he had ridden the track 16 times, reaching a maximum of 35 g-forces.

Stapp continued as a live subject on this and the high-speed track at Holloman Air Force Base in New Mexico. He performed his last deceleration test on December 10, 1954, from a velocity of 937 feet per second in 1.4 seconds, or 42.2 gs. Stapp also volunteered for a windblast test. The rear canopy of a Northrop F-89 Scorpion was cut away to expose the rear seat to the direct airstream. With Stapp in the rear cockpit, the ship was taken up to 35,000 feet in altitude and put into a steep dive. In this test, Stapp survived at a speed of 570 miles per hour.

These tests took their toll on Stapp's body. He sustained several broken ribs, a broken wrist, concussions, hernias, and permanent eye damage. But the results were the perfection of the design of aircraft restraint harnesses and establishing that the human body could sustain the deceleration gs, high-speed windblast, and high-altitude conditions that could be expected while ejecting from high-performance aircraft.

U.S. Air Force Col. A. M. "Chic" Henderson

U.S. Air Force Col. A. M. "Chic" Henderson volunteered to test a downward ejecting seat. An early Boeing B-47 Stratojet was modified to replace the standard non-ejecting seat at the bombardier/navigator's station with a downward ejection seat. Wearing a David Clark T-1 partial-pressure suit, Henderson ejected at an altitude of 10,000 feet at an indicated airspeed of 200 knots on December 7, 1953. The test took place over Elgin Air Force Base in Florida and was the world's first live downward ejection seat test. This was followed by downward ejection tests from the same aircraft by U.S. Air Force Capt. Ed Sperry, U.S. Air Force Lt. Hank Nielsen, and U.S. Air Force M.Sgt. George Post. The first and subsequent six tests were successful, except for the typical problem of seats of that period: injuries due to flailing arms and legs.

U.S. Air Force Capt. Joseph Kittinger Jr.

Kittinger soloed as a civilian in a Piper Cub and joined the U.S. Air Force where he graduated as a pilot with the rank of second lieutenant in 1950. He served overseas and then volunteered for zero-gravity testing followed by high-altitude parachute jump testing. This culminated in a balloon-supported open gondola in a program called Excelsior III. From this, Kittinger jumped at an altitude of 102,800 feet on August 16, 1960, wearing a David Clark MC-3 partial-pressure suit, plus heated gloves, socks, and a parka. The balloon liftoff took place at 5:29 A.M. near the town of Tularosa, about 18 miles from Holloman, New Mexico.

At 7:10 A.M. Kittinger stepped out of the gondola; 16 seconds later the timer deployed a pilot chute, which in turn deployed a 3-foot stabilization chute. By the time Kittinger had dropped to an altitude of 40,000 feet, the surrounding air temperature had dropped to 98 degrees below zero and he had attained a terminal velocity of 702 miles per hour. At 18,000 feet the aneroid pulled the pins and his main parachute—which measured 28 feet in diameter—opened. Twelve minutes and 32 seconds after Kittinger had stepped out of the gondola, he was safely back on Earth. This high-altitude parachute jump proved the operation of the Beaupre Multi-Stage Parachute (BMSP). A variation of this system later became the standard parachute system used in the high-altitude flights made by the Lockheed A-12 and SR-71 Blackbird.

Francis F. Beaupre

Francis F. Beaupre spent 2-1/2 years during World War II with the U.S. Navy as a parachute rigger and then joined WADC as a civilian. It was here that he developed the BMSP. Beaupre was not a college graduate but he had an innate talent for engineering. U.S. Air Force Col. John Stapp became his mentor, and through Stapp's efforts WADC finally accepted the parachute system that Beaupre had designed. This system provided timed opening of an 18-inch pilot chute, which pulled out a drogue chute that partially deployed the main parachute. At 18,000 feet an aneroid device allowed full inflation of the 28-inch-diameter main chute. After being proved in operation by Capt. Joseph Kittinger Jr. on August 16, 1960, a modification of this parachute system was used by pilots flying the Lockheed A-12 and SR-71.

U.S. Air Force Reserve Maj. James C. Hall

U.S. Air Force Reserve Major Hall was a professional parachute instructor. On October 1, 1965, Hall became the first human subject to successfully eject from the ground in a zero altitude/zero velocity condition in an American-built production ejection seat. This ejection took place in Los Angeles using a Weber Aircraft seat designed for the Convair F-106 Delta Dart fighter-interceptor— the media was in full attendance.

The Weber seat was mounted on a platform, which was staked to the ground. Within one second after Hall squeezed the ejection trigger, the 4,500-pound thrust from the rocket

U.S. Air Force Reserve Maj. James C. Hall, a professional parachute instructor, became the first human to successfully eject from the ground in a zero altitude/zero velocity condition in a U.S.-built production ejection seat. *Weber Aircraft, via Hal Watson*

catapult had pushed him to 400 feet in altitude and the man–seat separation had begun; two seconds later he was under a fully inflated parachute. The test was conducted adjacent to a lake behind Hansen Dam, and as Hall was descending, his survival kit was automatically deployed to drop down on a tether. By the time Hall descended into the water, his life raft had automatically inflated and was ready for his use. Both Hall and Weber Aircraft must have had great confidence in the system to invite the press to witness this first human demonstration.

The David Clark Co.

David M. Clark was employed as a knitter and worked in various textile plants. He had an idea for a new type of elastic fabric; in 1934 he scraped together $3,000 to buy a knitting machine and set it up in a rented space in a factory. His company flourished with the manufacture of brassieres and corsets. With the start of World War II, he expanded his business into products for the military. He worked with the U.S. Navy and U.S. Air Force, where he designed and manufactured many military items, including anti-g suits. Once again he expanded as he worked with the Navy, Air Force, and NASA in designing partial-pressure and full-pressure suits. Not only were these suits used in a broad range of production military aircraft, they were also used in many research aircraft. The NASA/Clark MC-2 was used in the NAA X-15, research aircraft, the U.S. Air Force/Clark S-100 used in the Lockheed U-2C, the U.S. Air Force/Clark S-970 used in the Lockheed A-12, and the U.S. Air Force/Clark S-901J and S-1030 used on the Lockheed SR-71. In addition to aircraft, David Clark's pressure suits were used in many of NASA's space vehicles. One would have to agree that a product line that covered the spectrum of bras to space suits extends to quite a range.

The Rocket Catapult

The later catapults used in Germany, Sweden, and early Britain and American ejection seats were all powered by explosive devices, some the equivalent of a blank 37-millimeter shell. While these types of devices could eject a pilot from his aircraft, the rapid g-force buildup resulted in many spinal injuries to ejection-seat users. Also, due to the rapid-burning (short-duration) characteristics of this type of catapult, it was unable to provide zero altitude/zero velocity ejection capability. Both the U.S. Army and Navy were seeking a solution to the problem.

The Mark 16 catapult, used on several versions of the Douglas Escapac, was primarily used by the U.S. Navy on the Lockheed Aircraft S-3 Viking antisubmarine and A-4 Skyhawk attack aircraft. *Universal Propulsion Company*

The solution began with a Rhodes scholar named Charles Bartley, employed by Jet Propulsion Laboratories (JPL) of Cal Tech. With the financial backing of Frank Marion, Bartley quit JPL and started Grand Central Rocket in Mentone, California. It was here that Bartley developed a composite rubber-based solid propellant, which made the rocket catapult practical.

In 1955, the Army Frankfort Arsenal contracted with Reaction Motors, Inc., of New Jersey, to develop a rocket-assisted ejection-seat catapult. However, the program was terminated prior to a successful test. Gerry Hirt, who had left

Frankfort Arsenal in 1954 and joined Talco Engineering Co. in Hamden, Connecticut, was the principal inventor of the rocket catapult, with a patent issued to Talco. The first rocket catapult carried part number PN 1057-2 and was first used to upgrade the U.S. Air Force Convair F-102 Delta Dagger ejection seat.

In almost the identical time frame, the U.S. Navy was also looking for a rocket catapult. In 1956, the Navy's Bureau of Aeronautics directed the Naval Ordinance Test Station (NOTS) in China Lake, California, to develop a catapult suitable for use in zero altitude/zero gravity situations. NOTS was successful in designing a catapult called Rocket Assisted Personnel Ejection Catapult (RAPEC). This catapult was first introduced on the production Douglas Aircraft A-4 Skyhawks. Both the Talco Engineering Co. and U.S. Navy RAPEC rocket catapults provided two important features: the thrust level was such that it minimized spinal damage to the occupant and, through its sustained burning time, was able to provide higher seat trajectories, making zero altitude/zero velocity seats possible.

These catapults can best be described as two-phase systems: the first phase is a gas-powered booster phase and the second a rocket-powered phase. System operation began with

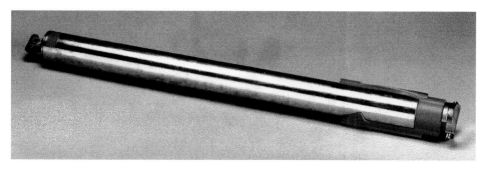

The Douglas Aircraft ACES II ejection seats utilized the CKU-5 catapults. *Universal Propulsion Company*

the pilot pulling down his face screen or pulling his ejection handle, which jettisoned the canopy and pulled the catapult sear pin. Following is a detailed description of the operation of the RAPEC catapult, which had a number of steps, all occurring in fractions of seconds.

Operation of the RAPEC Catapult

Pulling the sear pin released a spring-loaded firing pin, which struck the primer and ignited a percussion-sensitive powder, which in turn ignited boron potassium nitrate pellets. The pressure generated from the burning pellets ruptured the igniter case, allowing hot gases to enter the booster tube. The hot gases entering the booster tube ignited the booster charge, which was made of two strips of high-energy X-12 and one strip of N-5. The resulting pressure freed the motor and man–seat mass, which moved up the launcher tube. As the launcher tube exited, a port on the forward end of the booster tube was opened, igniting a zirconium lead-oxide igniter. This, in turn, initiated the High Energy X-12 propellant sustainer grain, imparting 4,200 pounds of thrust. The thrusting catapult pushed the man-seat the distance required for man–seat separation and to a safe altitude for automatic deployment of his parachute.

Due to the proven success of the rocket catapult, it became the standard for ejection seats around the world. The original Talco Engineering Co. rocket motors were built by Thiokol Chemical, using Bartley's polysulfide rubber-based propellant. When Rocket Power, Inc., and Talco Engineering joined forces, they began casting their own rocket motors with ever improving propellants. These motors became the catapults used in ejection seats built for the U.S. Air Force and some U.S. Navy aircraft. The RAPEC catapult became the core of Douglas Aircraft ejection seats, initially called Escapac and later named ACES II.

Shown here is an upper-end Rocket Assisted Personal Ejection Catapult (RAPEC) with a section cut away to expose its interior. Pulling the sear pin allows a spring-loaded firing pin to begin the ignition process. *John Dzurica*

At this point an odd situation arose. From the beginning, Martin-Baker in England and the U.S. Navy had formed a close working relationship. So it was natural for the Navy to share this new rocket catapult success with Martin-Baker. In the fall of 1957, Bill Thomas, a Navy Bureau of Aeronautics manager, attempted to interest Martin-Baker in the advantages offered by the RAPEC rocket catapult. At the time, Martin-Baker showed little interest in this ingenious device. It is possible that Martin-Baker was suffering from the NIH (Not Invented Here) syndrome, which has infected many companies over the years. Simplified, NIH generally means if "we" haven't thought of it, it's probably not needed or the correct way to approach the problem. Martin-Baker finally accepted the rocket catapult and demonstrated a prototype to the media on April 1, 1961. During this demonstration, Doddy Hay performed a zero altitude/zero gravity ejection, but with a catapult of Martin-Baker's own design.

Aneroid Automatic Parachute Deployment

On January 26, 1932, Leslie Irvin of the Irving Air Chute Company was issued a patent for an automatic parachute deployment device (through a clerical error, Irvin was misspelled as Irving). In this, the original form, the device was of a wind-down mechanism, which automatically deployed the parachute after six seconds. While six seconds was the recommended setting, it could be set to operate anywhere from two or more seconds. The purpose of the time delay was to make sure the parachutist was clear of the aircraft prior to deployment of his parachute. In modern high-speed aircraft, the time delay also allows the aerodynamic drag imposed upon the airman to slow his speed, thereby minimizing the opening shock load on the airman and the parachute.

Later, Leslie Irvin improved his device to include an automatic parachute release and his patent was revised to include this feature. The purpose of the barometric actuation was to prevent the parachute opening at altitudes where there was insufficient oxygen and atmospheric pressure to allow a parachutist to breathe. The barometric automatic activation devices are normally set to operate somewhere between 12,000 and 15,000 feet in altitude. The delay in opening the parachute until lower altitudes were reached also protected the parachutist from remaining in the extreme low temperatures, experienced at high altitudes, any longer than necessary.

When originally introduced, and in today's sport parachuting, the automatic devices were tied directly into the parachutist's harness. With the advent of ejection seats, crew escape modules, encapsulated seats, and the like, the devices are incorporated directly into the escape system. The mechanical force to actually deploy the parachute is generally either by a spring or a pyrotechnic device. The aneroid parachute deployment was a major step in the success of the automatic ejection seat. It also worked in synchronization with the rocket catapult to make zero altitude/zero velocity ejection seats possible. In the industry, these devices are either called Automatic Opening Devices (AOD) or, more recently, Automatic Activation Devices (AAD).

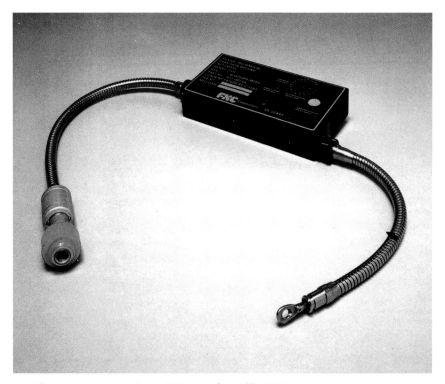

This Automatic Activation Device (AAD), manufactured by FXC Corporation, contains a barometric device that can be preset in 500-foot increments from sea level to 20,000 feet. It also contains a wind-down activation delay of zero through 8 seconds in 0.25-second increments. This AAD provides a force of 100 pounds to pull the parachute ripcord.
FXC Corporation

Chapter Seven

DOWNWARD EJECTION SEATS

Downward ejection seats came into being for several reasons. The main purpose was to allow crew members located in the lower side (bottom) of the aircraft a clear path for ejection. A secondary purpose was to provide post-ejection clearances between canopies/hatches and crew members and their ejection seats while ejecting from a multiplace aircraft.

U.S. Army Air Corps/Vultee XP-54 Swoose Goose

The U.S. Army Air Corps awarded Vultee a contract for two experimental high-altitude interceptors. The ships were designated as the XP-54, carrying Vultee Model Number 84, and nicknamed the Swoose Goose. This was a twin-boom, single-seat, pressurized-cockpit, pusher-type aircraft with tricycle landing gear. The aircraft had unusually long landing-gear struts to provide adequate propeller/ground clearance from

The Vultee XP-54 Swoose Goose, a pusher-type, high-altitude interceptor, raised and lowered the pilot into and out of his seat via an electric motor. For an event necessitating an in-flight escape, the pilot depressurized the cockpit and depressed a treadle, which manually rotated the seat down into the airstream below the level of the ship's pusher propeller. The seat harness was subsequently disconnected and the pilot would pull his D ring to deploy the parachute. *Vultee, via Nowell Ford*

the aft-mounted propeller when rotating for takeoff. This resulted in the lower side of the fuselage being quite high from the ground. Vultee engineers turned this into an asset.

The Air Corps and Vultee were both aware of the difficulty of exiting high-performance aircraft in the event of an emergency. So they chose to utilize a downward ejection seat. With the fuselage of the XP-54 so high off the ground it would have normally required a ladder for access to the cockpit. Instead, they chose to combine a downward ejection seat and a cockpit elevator into one unit. Thus, for the pilot to enter the cockpit, he sat in his seat—suspended below the aircraft—pushed a button, and was rotated up into his normal seating position within the aircraft. This procedure was reversed to exit the aircraft.

Ship number one (S/N 41-1210) was first flown from Muroc Army Air Base in Muroc, California, on January 15, 1943, by Vultee test pilot Frank W. Davis. After being flight-tested a little over 63 hours, it was flown to Wright Field, Ohio. Ship number two was only flown once, on May 24, 1944, from its manufacturer's plant in Downey, California, to Norton Army Air Base, California. Here, its gun nose was disassembled and shipped to Eglin Field, Florida, for testing.

Let's examine how the Vultee ejection seat worked. As this was to be a bottom-bailout aircraft, the pilot's control wheel was designed as a yoke, crossing above his legs, pivoting on both sides of the cockpit. This eliminated any objects in his path during the time of downward ejection. To eject, the pilot merely pulled a handle on the right side of his seat, which dumped the cabin pressure and armed the system. He then pressed down with both feet on a treadle bar, and the automatic sequence began. This resulted in the pilot rotating down and out to where his seat harness was automatically released. This position took the pilot well clear of the propeller. At that point, he would manually pull his ripcord to continue with a normal parachute descent.

The Convair XP-54 Swoose Goose high-altitude interceptor-fighter provided the pilot with a nonpowered, downward ejection seat.
1) The pilot depressurizes the cockpit and pushes his toes against the foot treadle to initiate the automatic ejection sequence.
2) The pilot's seat rotates down into the airstream.
3) The seat harness is automatically released and the pilot rotates down clear of the propeller arc, where he manually pulls his parachute D ring to deploy his parachute.
Convair, via Dusty Rhodes

It turned out that the XP-54's escape system was never used. As this seat utilized gravity to effect ejection, this naturally required the aircraft to be upright and somewhat stable to eject. Many times, however, these are not the conditions that exist when a pilot has to abandon an aircraft, and could have been a big liability. The return to downward ejection seats would have to wait another 14 years.

U.S. Air Force/Boeing Airplane Co.
B-47 Stratojet Bomber

The first flight of the Boeing Airplane Co. XB-47 bomber (Boeing Model 203) (S/N 46-65) took place on December 17, 1947. The flight was made from Boeing Field in Seattle, piloted by Robert Robbins with copilot Scott Osler. The pilot's and copilot's seats were upward ejecting. In the early B-47s, the navigator was not provided with an ejection seat and had to manually bail out. Part of the reason the navigator was not provided with an ejection seat was the concern about post-ejection collisions between crew members.

WADC was also concerned about spinal injuries to crew members, especially with the ejection forces required to catapult crew members over aircraft with tall vertical stabilizers, such as the B-47. If a downward ejecting system were used the catapult forces could be reduced, as the seat would be working with gravity. Thus in 1952, Wright Field approved the development of a downward ejecting seat. Due to successful live tests of a downward ejection seat, the design was incorporated into production B-47 aircraft; both Republic and Weber Aircraft manufactured these seats. Another interesting feature of the escape system on the B-47 had to do with the copilot's upward ejection seat, built by Weber Aircraft. The copilot also functioned as a tail gunner, using a radar gun sight. To operate this sight, the copilot's ejection seat was mounted on a swivel. To operate the tail gun, he would turn his seat 180 degrees to the aft and look into a radar screen. This special seat assembly required the copilot to rotate his seat forward to eject.

U.S. Air Force/Douglas X-3 Stiletto Research Aircraft

The Douglas X-3 Stiletto was a joint U.S. Air Force/U.S. Navy/National Advisory Committee for Aeronautics single-place, twin-engine research aircraft to study the transonic speed range. The Stiletto (S/N 49-2892) was first flown from Edwards Air Force Base in California by Douglas test pilot William B. Bridgeman on October 20, 1952. The Stiletto utilized a Douglas-built, boom-stabilized downward ejecting seat, which was successfully tested at supersonic speeds. In the event the pilot had to eject, the sequence was completely automatic once the pilot jettisoned the door and activated his ejection handle.

The Douglas Aircraft Stilleto was a single-place, twin-engine experimental research aircraft and was equipped with a Douglas downward ejection seat. This aircraft is presently on display at the U.S. Air Force Museum in Dayton, Ohio. *Boeing Historical Archives*

The configuration of the Stiletto's windshield would have made cockpit ingress and egress quite difficult. So instead, Douglas integrated its downward ejection seat into an elevator for ground entry and exit. An electric motor was integrated with the ejection seat so that on the ground the seat could

Douglas Aircraft integrated its downward ejection seat with an entry and exit elevator on the X-3 research aircraft. Drawing by Douglas Aircraft

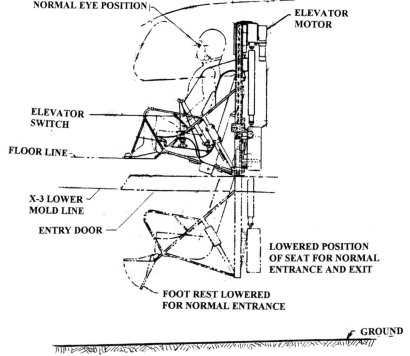

NORMAL EYE POSITION

ELEVATOR MOTOR

ELEVATOR SWITCH

FLOOR LINE

X-3 LOWER MOLD LINE

ENTRY DOOR

LOWERED POSITION OF SEAT FOR NORMAL ENTRANCE AND EXIT

FOOT REST LOWERED FOR NORMAL ENTRANCE

GROUND

Douglas Aircraft integrated its downward ejection seat with an entry and exit elevator on the Stiletto X-3 research aircraft. *Douglas Aircraft, via Boeing Historical Archives*

be lowered or raised on a set of rails from the bottom of the aircraft. To enter the aircraft, the pilot would sit in the extended seat, and by actuating an electric switch, the motor would raise him up into his normal flight position. Normal ground egress was accomplished by reversing the procedure.

The downward ejection seat of the Douglas Aircraft X-3 Stiletto also served as an elevator to allow the pilot access to the cockpit. *Boeing Historical Archives*

In the event a wheels-up landing was made, the pilot could exit the aircraft by opening his cockpit's side window. The flight-testing of the Stiletto never required the use of its downward ejection seat nor escape from its cockpit side window. The Douglas X-3 Stiletto is on display at The Air Force Museum in Dayton, Ohio.

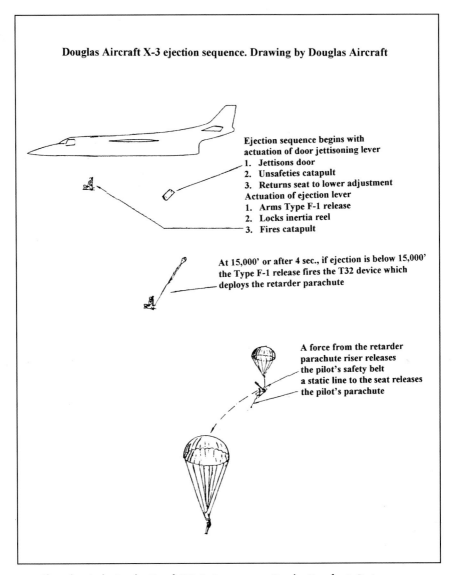

Douglas Aircraft X-3 ejection sequence. Drawing by Douglas Aircraft

Ejection sequence begins with
actuation of door jettisoning lever
1. Jettisons door
2. Unsafeties catapult
3. Returns seat to lower adjustment
Actuation of ejection lever
1. Arms Type F-1 release
2. Locks inertia reel
3. Fires catapult

At 15,000' or after 4 sec., if ejection is below 15,000'
the Type F-1 release fires the T32 device which
deploys the retarder parachute

A force from the retarder
parachute riser releases
the pilot's safety belt
a static line to the seat releases
the pilot's parachute

Shown here is the Douglas Aircraft X-3 ejection sequence. *Douglas Aircraft, via Boeing Historical Archives*

Shown here is a Douglas downward ejection seat after an in-flight test. The seat not only performed as designed, but survived with little damage. *Boeing Historical Archives*

U.S. Air Force/Lockheed F-104 Starfighter Fighter

The Lockheed Starfighter was a single-place, single-engine, low-wing Mach 2 fighter. X-104 (S/N 53-7786) was first flown on February 7, 1954, from Edwards Air Force Base in California by Lockheed test pilot Anthony W. LeVier. During its preliminary design phase, an ejectable nose escape system was studied, but then the F-104 was designed to utilize a Stanley A downward ejection seat. On February 17, 1956, the first of several YF-104As built was flown. Several were lost due to engine failure just after takeoff, which resulted in the loss of the aircraft and their pilots. Because of this, the aircraft and its seat were redesigned to become upward ejecting, and now utilize a Stanley C ejection seat.

Originally fitted with a Stanley Aviation downward ejection seat, the Lockheed F-104 Starfighter was redesigned and equipped with an upward ejection seat. *Lockheed Martin Skunk Works*

U.S. Air Force/Douglas Aircraft RB-66A
Destroyer Reconnaissance

The Douglas RB-66A Destroyer (S/N 52-2828) was first flown on June 28, 1954, from Long Beach Municipal Airport in Long Beach, California. The pilot for this flight was George Jansen. The three-man crew had a combination of upward and downward ejection seats. The upward seats were built by Aircraft Mechanics, and Stanley Aviation built the downward seats.

U.S. Air Force/North American Aviation
YF-107A Fighter-Bomber

NAA Model No. 212, YF-107A, was a single-place, low-wing, single-engine, Mach 2.0 fighter-bomber. The ship (C/N 212-1, S/N 55-5118) was first flown on September 10, 1956, by NAA test pilot Robert Baker from Edwards Air Force Base in California. The YF-107A had an unusual air-intake location for its J79 jet engine—on the topside of the fuselage, just aft of the cockpit. A number of reasons led to this inlet position, including the need for a nose-mounted radar, the requirement for a central armament store location under the wing, and a smooth, stable airflow for its engine inlet control system. This inlet location also reduced the possibilities of engine foreign object problems. Foreign object problems usually occurred during high engine thrust levels during takeoff, which suck up runway debris—a very critical time of flight to lose an engine!

The North American Aviation F-107A, with its engine air intake directly above and aft of the cockpit, posed special challenges in creating an upward ejection seat. Originally designed with a downward ejection seat, the design eventually evolved into using an upward ejection seat. *North American Aviation*

Prior studies done by Boeing on their B-47 and Douglas on their X-3 showed that it was easier to introduce the seat into a high-speed airstream by downward—rather than upward—ejection. This benefit, together with the concern about ejecting in front of the powerful suction of the engine inlet, tipped the scales to influence the Air Force and NAA to select an open-faced, downward ejecting seat with a fixed canopy. The downward ejection seat would also act as an elevator, to raise or lower the pilot into or out of the cockpit.

Due to the injuries sustained from the supersonic bailout of NAA production test pilot George Smith in an F-100, it was decided that the maximum safe ejection envelope would be Mach 0.89. In the event of an emergency occurring above this speed, the pilot would have to reduce his airspeed to within the safe limits or accept the chance of injuries during ejection.

NAA's Advanced Design Group was about ready to release the drawings to engineering's basic design groups. At about the same time, NAA learned of the problems that Lockheed was having with its downward ejection seat in the F-104 and decided to revert to an upward ejection seat. Lockheed later redesigned the F-104 to use an upward ejection seat. This redirection was not a simple task, as it required the redesign of the fixed cockpit canopy to be openable for ingress and egress, plus to be ballistically removed as part of the ejection sequence.

There was great concern about the ability of an upward ejecting seat to get the pilot safely past the engine inlet. The system that evolved was typical of the time: an automatic ejection seat with a rocket catapult. Ejection seat stabilization in the airstream was accomplished by the use of a ribbon drogue chute attached to each of the ballistically extended arms on each side of the headrest.

Due to the concern of ejecting in front of the engine inlet, great attention was focused on the early sled testing. In a test at the U.S. Air Force high-speed track facilities at Edwards Air Force Base in California, the ejection seat was mounted on an abbreviated F-107 forward fuselage. With the cameras whirring and many eyewitnesses in attendance, it appeared that the fears were well founded. As the ejection seat emerged from the cockpit, its stabilization arms extended with the seat bent or tilted rearward into the engine inlet duct structure. Both the seat and engine inlet were severely damaged.

As was typical, an anthropomorphic dummy (nick-named "Sierra Sam") was in the ejection seat. The test was being performed only to check the seat's ability to clear the engine inlet, and not to test the remainder of the ejection sequence. Thus Sierra Sam's legs had been tied to the ejection seat's foot stirrups with nylon rope. The aerodynamic forces were so powerful that the nylon leg ropes broke and the dummy was literally split up the middle. The test appeared to show a complete failure of the planned ejection system, that was, until the test track telemetry revealed that the sled was not traveling at the programmed Mach 0.89 but somewhat above Mach 1.2.

The test sleds were propelled along the track by several solid rocket motors designed to fire in a series. On this test, the rocket sequence was designed to maintain the test sled at Mach 0.89 as it traveled through the section of track called the "test window," or "trap." Instead of a series of rocket thrust pulses, several rockets ignited simultaneously, push-ing the sled considerably beyond the desired speed. Even though the problem had been caused by excessive sled speeds, on subsequent tests the ejection seat rails were extended slightly. With this change incorporated, the ejection seat had no problem clearing the inlet and it was certi-fied for use. Republic won the production contract with their F-105 and only three prototype YF-107As were built. The need to eject never arose.

Chapter Eight

MULTI-MODE ESCAPE SYSTEMS

Many aircraft had crews consisting of several members. Crew arrangement within these aircraft sometimes prevented a single type of crew-escape system to be used. Thus, escape system solutions were almost as varied as the aircraft themselves.

U.S. Army Air Corps/North American Aviation B-45 Tornado Bomber

The inaugural flight of the NAA XB-45 Tornado bomber (NAA Model NA-130, AF S/N 45-59479) took place on March 17, 1947, from Muroc Army Air Field in Muroc, California. The pilot for the maiden flight was George Krebs, assisted by flight-test engineer Paul Brewer. The B-45 was a four-place aircraft, with the pilot and copilot provided with ejection

106

seats. The bombardier/navigator and tail gunner had to use the typical World War II escape system of over-the-side bailouts with manual parachutes. This approach established a first-class/second-class flight crew relationship on the 142 Tornados built.

North American Aviation's B-45 Tornado was originally a four-place, four-engine bomber. The pilot and copilot were equipped with upward ejection seats, and the bombardier/navigator and tail gunner were forced to rely on over-the-side bailouts. *North American Aviation*

U.S. Air Force/Boeing Airplane Co.
B-47 Stratojet Bomber

The first flight of the Boeing XB-47 Stratojet bomber (Boeing Model 303, S/N 46-65) was made by Robert Robbins as pilot, assisted by Scott Osler as copilot. The flight took place on December 17, 1947, from Boeing Field in Seattle. The pilot and copilot were provided with ejection seats, while on the early models the bombardier/navigator had to escape using his own parachute in an over-the-side technique. A total of 2,031 Stratojets were built, with the later models providing a downward ejection seat for the bombardier/navigator.

U.S. Air Force/Boeing Airplane Co.
B-52 Stratofortress Bomber

The initial flight of the Boeing Airplane Co. YB-52 Stratofortress bomber (Boeing Model 464, AF S/N 49-231) took place on April 15, 1952. The flight was made from Boeing Field in Seattle and was piloted by Alvin "Tex" Johnston with U.S. Air Force Lt. Col. Guy Townsend as copilot. The B-52 had a mixture of upward and downward ejection seats. Unfortunately, instructors were often carried onboard and were not provided with ejection seats. This was a serious problem and was compounded by the escape path for these men. In the event an in-flight escape were required, the instructors had to await the downward ejection of the navigator. After the

The Boeing B-52 Stratofortress had upward and downward ejection seats, although instructors and gunners relied on typical over-the-side bailouts. *Boeing Historical Archives*

navigator had ejected, this provided an opening in the floor so the instructors could make over-the-side manual bailouts.

The multi-mode escape system used on the B-52 had several disadvantages. Because the takeoff phase of flight is generally the most hazardous, the engines are under the maximum stress and thus more likely to fail than at any other time. If the decision to eject occurred just after takeoff, the downward ejection seats would most probably result in the death of crew members using them. The same thing is true with those crew members who have to use the over-the-side bailout technique. There would be insufficient altitude to effectively deploy a parachute for a safe landing.

B-52s were involved in many bombing raids over Vietnam. This was an extremely dangerous flying environment, due to Russian surface-to-air missiles (SAMs). The aircrews flying these missions bonded into close-knit groups. In the event that escape was required from a damaged aircraft, it was difficult for those seated in ejection seats knowing that their comrades would have to struggle through a manual bailout. Another factor entering into this equation is that the instructors were generally the senior officers onboard the aircraft. It is a fact that some B-52 crewmen were lost while awaiting their non-ejection–equipped crew members to manually bail out. The last model of the 744 Stratofortresses built was the B-52H, which is still in active duty today.

Weber built both the upward and downward ejection seats.

Rockwell International B-1 Bomber

The B-1 bomber (B-1A, ship No. 4 and B-1B Lancers) was a four-place aircraft, with provisions for two instructors. The first of these four-engined bombers was the B-1A (S/N 76-0174), which was first flown from Palmdale Airport in Palmdale, California, on February 14, 1979. The pilot was Rockwell Chief Test Pilot Mervin L. Evenson; the copilot was

U.S. Air Force Lt. Col. Fred Fiedler; U.S. Air Force Maj. E. V. Dyer was the offensive system operator (OSO); and the flight-test engineer was Rockwell's Dave Mirgon. The first of the 100 Lancers built was B-1B (S/N 82-0001), which was also flown from Palmdale Airport, this time on October 18, 1984. The pilot was Evenson, with U.S. Air Force Lt. Col. Leroy Schroeder as copilot; Maj. Stephen A. Henry was the OSO; and Capt. David Hamilton Jr. was the flight-test engineer.

The four crew members (pilot, copilot, OSO, and defensive system operator [DSO]) were seated in Douglas ACES II ejection seats. Each of the four had a two-mode selector with positions of manual or auto. In the auto mode, when either the pilot or copilot ejected, the other three seats were automatically ejected. In the manual mode, the seats operated independently.

In addition to the four-man crew, the aircraft had provisions for two instructors in stowable seats. In the event escape became necessary, the instructors would don personal

The Rockwell International B-1B Lancer bomber was equipped with ACES II ejection seats built by Weber Aircraft. *Boeing Historical Archives*

parachutes. The instructors then pulled a handle, which had several functions: the crew cabin was decompressed, the nose landing gear was lowered (providing an airstream deflector), and pyrotechnics jettisoned the outer entry ladder and door. Opening the inner cabin door, the crew would drop out the bottom of the aircraft and manually deploy their own parachutes. All of this was a time-consuming process, especially if the need to eject were imminent.

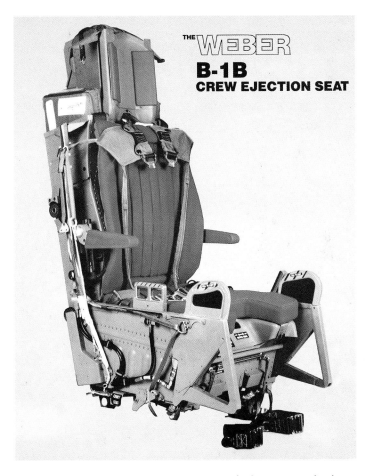

The Aces II ejection seat was designed by Douglas Aircraft. The B-1B Lancer bomber was equipped with this seat, built by Weber Aircraft. *Weber Aircraft*

Chapter Nine

JETTISONABLE NOSES

The purpose of an escape system utilizing an ejectable nose was to protect the airmen from entering a turbulent airstream if ejecting during high-speed flight. In the post-ejection sequence, after the ejectable nose had slowed, the airman would exit the nose and manually open his parachute.

German Heinkel He-176 Rocket Fighter

The Heinkel He-176 was a single-place, midwing, rocket-powered experimental aircraft, whose design by Hans Regner began in late 1937. The aircraft was of minimal size, designed essentially to a size to fit its projected pilot, Erich Warsitz. To reduce aerodynamic drag, the pilot sat in a slightly reclined position, much as can be seen in some of today's fighters, such as the Lockheed F-16. In addition to the He-176 being rocket-powered, another unique feature was that its pilot was provided with a jettisonable nose, which was separated from the aircraft by compressed air. To reduce the opening loads on its drogue chute, a timer delayed its opening, allowing aerodynamic drag to take effect. After that, its pilot would jettison his cockpit canopy, bail out in a conventional manner, and then deploy his own parachute.

The Heinkel He-176 rocket-powered fighter had a jettisonable-nose escape system. *Heinkel*

On June 30, 1939, Erich Warsitz made the first flight of the He-176, from Usedom Island, Germany, for a flight that lasted about 30 seconds and ended in a smooth landing. Airborne testing showed the jettisonable nose had a serious drawback. In a series of tests, a Heinkel He-111 carried a He-176 test nose, with a dummy in its cockpit, to different altitudes, where the nose was dropped. From these tests it was determined that a minimum altitude of 19,680 feet was required for the drogue chute to function, the pilot to exit the nose and manually deploy his parachute, and to assure that the parachute canopy fully inflated. It was not reasonable to assume that a pilot would have this altitude available every time, so this was an unacceptable escape solution.

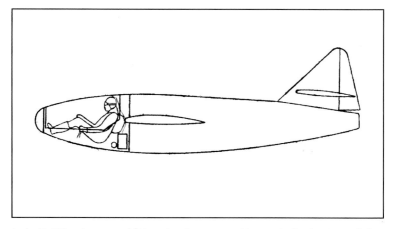

In the He-176 rocket-powered fighter, the pilot was seated in a semireclined position, which provided for an extremely smooth, aerodynamic nose. This position also provided the pilot the capability of withstanding more positive g-forces without blacking out. *Jim Tuttle*

The He-176 was flown many times, accident free, by a number of pilots, and was even demonstrated before Hitler. The aircraft structure was quite heavy, which resulted in high wing loading and poor performance. With the outbreak of World War II, the testing was ended with only the one ship being built. It was put on display in the Berlin Air Museum and subsequently lost in an Allied bombing raid during 1943.

U.S. Navy/Douglas D-558-2 Skyrocket Research Aircraft

Douglas Aircraft received a contract to build a single-place, turbojet, high-speed research aircraft designated as the D-558-2 Skyrocket. Douglas test pilot John F. Martin made the maiden flight (BuAer 37973) from Muroc Army Air Force Base in California. This flight took place on February 4, 1948. Due to the possibility of bailout at high speed, an ejectable-nose escape system was chosen for the aircraft. The ejectable-nose design effort was originally done for the D-558-1 Skystreak, but after a nose-engine inlet was chosen for the dash one, the design was incorporated into the dash two. If the need to escape arose on the D-558-2, the pilot pulled a handle, which released four bomb-rack-type hooks. This separated the nose from the remainder of the fuselage.

The Douglas Aircraft D-558-2 Skyrocket was equipped with an ejectable nose. This system was originally developed for the D-558-1 Skystreak, but it wasn't implemented until the birth of the D-558-2. *Douglas Aircraft, via Boeing Historical Archives*

Test pilot John F. Martin sits in the cockpit of a Douglas Aircraft D-558-2 Skyrocket. The ejectable nose is separated from the rest of the fuselage. *Douglas Aircraft, via Boeing Historical Archives*

Here, a test subject simulates escape from the ejectable nose of a Douglas Aircraft D-558-1, a system not implemented until the D-558-2. The test subject is wearing a backpack-type parachute. *Douglas Aircraft*

The separation phase was quite an engineering challenge, and included disconnecting electrical connectors; flight-control cabling; pitot static lines; and heating, cooling, and pressurization ducting, to name a few. Instead of relying on a drogue chute, the ejectable nose relied upon aerodynamic friction to stabilize and slow the nose. After the nose slowed sufficiently, the pilot opened a rear door on the cockpit, climbed out, and used his own personal parachute to bail out. The aircraft went through some power plant changes and was then reidentified as the D558-2. The need to use the jettisonable nose never arose on the D558-2.

After the D-558-1's nose was severed, the pilot would perform a manual bailout from the back of the nose section. To test this on the ground, a fixture was built and the test subject would attempt to perform manual bailouts from a number of positions.
Boeing History Archives

U.S. Air Force/NASA/Bell X-2 Experimental Research Aircraft

Bell Aircraft received a contract to build two advanced X-2 aircraft funded jointly by the U.S. Air Force and NASA. The X-2 was planned to expand the flight speed and altitude envelopes attained by the X-1 series. This required a more powerful rocket engine, improved aerodynamic shaping and K-monel, stainless-steel materials replacing some sections of aluminum, and a tinted, highly tempered windshield. Another major difference from the X-I series was that the X-2 was equipped with a unique escape system. In the event escape became necessary, the pressurized nose section was separated from the fuselage. This was accomplished with an explosive charge. A ribbon-type parachute would automatically deploy and stabilize the capsule as it dropped to an altitude at which the pilot could bail out in a normal manner.

This Bell Aircraft X-2 rocket research aircraft was equipped with a jettisonable nose. The plane and its pilot were lost in a high-speed-record attempt. *Air Force Flight Test Center History Department, Edwards Air Force Base*

JETTISONABLE NOSES

The first of these two ships was lost in an in-flight explosion. In May 1953, the X-2 was on a nonstop fueling test in its B-50 Superfortress Mother Ship over Lake Ontario. Three men were in the converted bomb bay, overseeing the X-2. Its pilot, Jean "Skip" Ziegler, was astride the X-2 when a large fire broke out from within the X-2. Jumping off the X-2, Ziegler yelled, "Drop the beast!" As it fell away from the B-50's bomb bay, a tremendous explosion from the X-2 blew Ziegler and Frank Wolko to their deaths. One other crewman was able to hang on until he could be pulled back into the B-50. Ziegler, Wolko, and the X-2 were never located.

Here the X-2's jettisonable nose is being attached to the aircraft. In the event of an in-flight escape, the nose was ejected. Once the nose-section altitude and speed were compatible, the pilot would make a conventional over-the-side parachute jump. *Bell Aircraft*

The second X-2 made its first powered flight on November 18, 1955, with U.S. Air Force Lt. Col. Pete Everest at the controls. On each subsequent flights, the X-2 was progressing and reaching higher speeds. As the ship attained higher speeds and

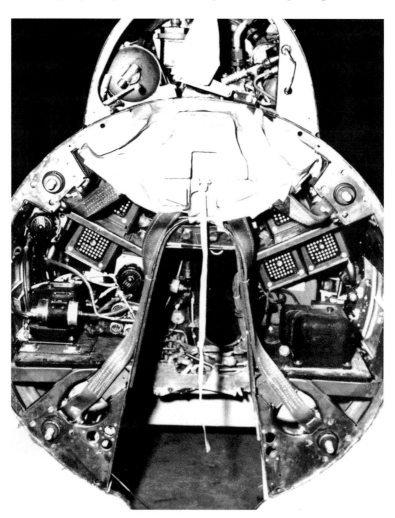

Shown here is the rear bulkhead of the ejectable nose for the Bell Aircraft X-2 rocket research aircraft. The nose was structurally connected to the remaining fuselage by the four large, equally spaced pins that are visible here. The heavy sections of webbing, near each pin, connected the nose to its port-ejection drogue chute. The heavy white section near the top of the nose was the drogue chute storage compartment. *Bell Aircraft*

greater altitudes, it was noted that in rare atmosphere the X-2 was less and less stable. The ailerons, elevator, and rudder became ineffective in the rarified air. Having reached Mach 2.87, the Air Force wanted to exceed Mach 3 before turning the ship over to NASA. It chose U.S. Air Force Capt. Milburn G. Apt to make this record attempt. Apt was given briefings by former X-2 pilots and spent time in the ground simulator, learning the X-2's flight characteristics.

Prior flight tests had shown that to attain Mach 3, it would require the pilot to follow a precise flight path. On September 18, 1955, the X-2 was carried to altitude by its B-50 and released to fly under rocket power. Apt maintained an almost perfect balance between the X-2's pitch angle and thrust. In addition, on this flight the rocket motor provided about 10 seconds of additional thrust and Apt did reach Mach 3. Then something went seriously wrong. Possibly thinking he was traveling too far away from Edwards Air Force Base, Apt made a rather abrupt turn back toward base, and the X-2 made a series of uncommanded diverging rolls and then went completely out of control. The aircraft motions were so violent that Apt was literally pounded into unconsciousness. The aircraft entered an inverted spin as the cockpit-recording camera continued running. On the film, Apt is seen to regain consciousness and attempt to stabilize the aircraft. Failing this, he decided to eject.

The fuselage jettisonable nose capsule was forced away and the drogue chute deployed, but instead of a safe haven, the capsule nose suddenly pitched down and took vengeance upon its already battered pilot. Apt was knocked unconscious, once again. The cockpit cameras showed Apt regaining consciousness and preparing to bail out as the nose capsule slammed into the desert floor, killing its valiant pilot. Meanwhile the, X-2 spun into the earth about 5 miles away. That was the last of the X-2s ever built.

Chapter Ten

Semi-Ejection Seats

In the early 1960s, the Stanley Aviation Corporation saw a need for a simple escape system that could be retrofitted into existing aircraft. The design that evolved was called the YANKEE. Unlike standard ejection seats, which pushed a crewman out of the aircraft literally by the seat of his pants, the YANKEE used a tractor rocket to pull (yank) the crewman from the aircraft. The crewman wore a harness quite similar to that of a standard parachute, except that it was connected by straps to a spin-stabilized tractor rocket, located behind him.

The ejection sequence was initiated by pulling a D-ring from between his knees. This jettisoned the canopy, the crewman's seat articulated with the seat pan rotating down, the seat back moved up a set of rails, released the crew member's five-point safety harness, and fired a catapult. This launched the rocket, which was ignited when the Perlon pendants—straps attached to the crewman—reached their limit of stretch. This action positioned the crewman in almost a standing position as the tractor rocket pulled him out of the cockpit. When the rocket had expended about 90 percent of its energy, the pendant lines were severed, allowing the almost-spent rocket and pendant lines to continue away. At this point, a drogue chute assisted in opening the parachute, which was forcibly spread, ballistically, by a second small rocket. This provided a safe descent from zero altitude and 30 knots up to about 250 knots.

While this design was not usable in high-performance aircraft, it provided something else quite important. With minimal rework this system could be installed in aircraft never designed for ejection seats. As the crewman using the YANKEE system was essentially standing as he was pulled from the aircraft, the normal canopy opening was sufficient in size and required only minimum rework—that being to effect its jettison.

The major use of the YANKEE system was during the Vietnam War. The retrofits were done primarily on Douglas Aircraft A-1E (two-place) and A-1H/J (single-place) Skyraiders.

The YANKEE System

The first of the 3,180 Skyraiders built was flown on March 18, 1945, as the XBT2D-1 from Los Angeles Municipal Airport by LeVelne W. Browne. In addition, a number of North American T-28 Trojans were also retrofitted with the YANKEE system. The first of the 1,948 T-28s built (S/N 48-1371) was first flown on September 24, 1949, from Los Angeles Municipal Airport. The pilot was Jean L. "Skip" Ziegler. The low-level attack and spotter missions, flown by Skyraiders and Trojans over Vietnam, were very dangerous work. It was under these conditions that the YANKEE was put to good use and saved many lives. In addition to its use in the A-1s and

T-28s, the YANKEE system was installed in a number of other aircraft. After Stanley Aviation left the field of escape systems, the license for the YANKEE system was sold to Stencel, where the system was sold as the Ranger. The license now resides with Universal Propulsion Company, a division of B.F. Goodrich Co.

The Douglas Aircraft A-1 Skyraider was a two-place attack aircraft used extensively in Vietnam. Due to the danger of their missions, Skyraiders were modified to include Stanley Aviation YANKEE semi-ejection seats. The Skyraider pictured is similar to the one used by Maj. Bill Bagwell and Maj. Pete Wilson over Vietnam. *Boeing Historical Archives*

A YANKEE Ejection, by Pete Williams

I was based in Thailand. On November 1, 1969, the day's mission was to be an armed reconnaissance flight into Northern Laos as the number-two aircraft in a flight of two.

The North American Aviation T-28 Trojan was a two-place trainer also used in Vietnam. Like the Skyraider, the Trojans' dangerous missions required it be retrofitted with the YANKEE escape system. *North American Aviation*

I was the instructor pilot in the right seat for a newly arrived pilot (also a major) in our squadron. The mission was to be his second combat mission and the first in-theatre, driving in the left seat. We were in a Douglas A1-E Skyraider S/N 13-2455, with a radio call sign of Firefly 27.

I don't recall the takeoff time, but think it was around 8:00 A.M. Our ordinance load was generic for the mission: mixed hard 500-pound bombs, napalm, and rockets, as I remember. Everything was normal on the takeoff: join up and climb out. We were cruising at around 9,000 feet, approximately 75 to 100 miles northwest of Nakhon Phanom (NKP), which was our home air base in Eastern Thailand, just across the river west of north central Laos. Just about then, we had a dramatic loss of power with accompanying smoke and flames around the engine cowl. We immediately turned to the south and attempted to get the engine going again, to no avail.

EJECT!

As we descended through 5,000 feet (about 3,500 to 4,000 AGL), I directed the pilot to initiate the extraction sequence and told him I'd be right behind him. I remember seeing him pull the seat extraction handle between his legs, and shortly thereafter I did the same. I have the impression that he had his hands under his chin with the handle firmly clenched and the lanyard hanging down. I also think that I could see the swaged ball at the end of the lanyard, without the clip that is, I think, removed to start the sequence by firing the primer cord around the canopy.

At any rate, at this time my extraction sequence began and the next thing I remember is the chute opening. I was aware that the pilot did not appear to get out of the aircraft. After the chute opened, I believe I was about 1,000 to 1,500 feet above the trees and turned the chute in an attempt to sight the aircraft. By this time, all I could see was the fireball where the aircraft impacted. I entered the trees, gathered my gear, and made my way to a small, more open area than where I came down. With my survival gear radio on guard channel, I got in touch with my flight leader in his A-1.

He had stayed on station, circling my area for about an hour, and then passed on some welcome information—Jolly Green 17 was approaching. Jolly Green was a rescue helicopter equipped with a forest penetrator (a folded metal cylinder about 4 feet high and 1 to 1-1/2 feet in diameter). I tried to use my survival mirror to alert the chopper as to my exact location, but the trees were too tall. The A-1 pilot knew where I was and vectored the chopper to my approximate position. When the chopper was directly overhead, I popped a smoke flare to provide my precise location and wind direction and the chopper then lowered the penetrator.

The penetrator hit the ground within 15 to 20 feet of my location. I went over to the penetrator, let it all the way to the ground, spread the three legs, and undid the safety belt. I then

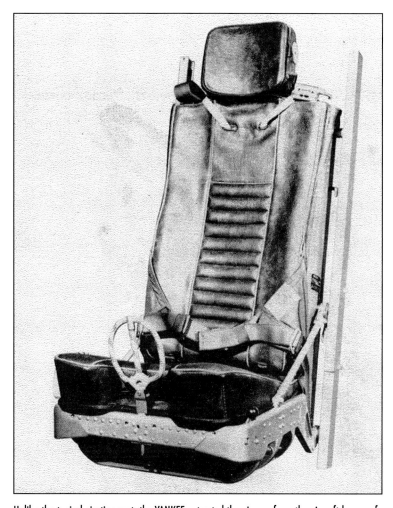

Unlike the typical ejection seat, the YANKEE extracted the airman from the aircraft by use of a tractor rocket. Ejection was initiated by pulling up on the D ring, seen at the front of the seat. During the initial steps of the sequence, the crewman's seat pan rotated down, while the seat back rose a few inches up a set of rails. This placed the crew in a near-standing position as the tractor rocket pulled the crew member from the aircraft. *Stanley Aviation*

straddled the legs with the penetrator held upright and the belt tightened around my waist and gave the thumbs-up.

The penetrator started up and, at about 50 feet or so, began to spin—slowly at first but with increasing revolutions.

The sensation wasn't too bad while I was still below the tree-tops, but once I was out of the trees and the chopper started slowly forward, I felt like I might pass out and fall off! I just closed my eyes, held on for dear life, and waited until I felt the floor of the chopper hit my fanny. The parajumper pulled me

TYPICAL
SEAT AND RAIL
ASSEMBLY

Notice the seat-pan mechanism on the left of this YANKEE installation diagram. On the right is the combination launcher and tractor rocket. Dual 12-foot nylon pendants connect between the airman's parachute harness and the launcher/tractor rocket. *Stanley Aviation*

aboard and away we went for NKP. The parajumpers were enlisted men who either came down on the penetrator to aid an injured airman or, as in my case, were the principle recovery contact—really great guys!

The cause of the accident was later determined to be engine failure. The pilot's ejection seat failed to operate and his body was recovered within a day or so. Other than some bumps and bruises from the ejection and crawling about on the jungle floor (I had moved about 1/2 to 3/4 mile) and the damnedest discoloration/bruising in the crotch area (where the leg straps fastened), I was uninjured. I stood-down the rest of November 1 and 2, but flew my next A-1H mission on November 3 as a "sandy" (search and rescue of downed aircrew).

Not Me Again! The Story of a Pilot Forced to Make a Second YANKEE Bailout, by Bill Bagwell

In June 1969, on what was to be my next-to-last combat sortie, Lt. Col. Bill Neal and I were scheduled to fly together with a new crewman, Capt. Rick Drury, as our wingman. Neal had just returned from R&R (rest and rehabilitation) in Hawaii, and our policy called for an instructor pilot to fly with him and recertify him for combat. We had been slated for a quiet area on what would have been a "milk run."

We were assigned the radio call sign of "Hobo" and had already started briefing when the operations officer came in and said we were being diverted to "Barrel Roll," the combat area in northern Laos. He said the North Vietnamese Army had crossed the Laotian border and assaulted and surrounded Mong Soui, a CIA base near the Plaines de Jarres (PDJ).

This was just one of the "other wars" in Laos. The PDJ was about the only area that was flat enough to support farming. It had changed hands any number of times, depending on the relative strength of the sides. Clearly, the bad guys wanted to occupy it just before the monsoon season so it would be too muddy for us to regain with a counteroffensive. As well, the CIA had just finished restocking Mong Soui so they would hold it themselves during the rainy season. The prize for both sides was the base and all the fresh supplies. This "other war" was a big deal because it would become a bargaining chip in the peace talks that were going on at the time.

Bill and I wasted no time getting the Douglas A-1E Skyraider ready. It was a two-seater with dual controls. Rick's plane had just come out of maintenance following extensive repairs. We all finally got airborne and headed north. Since one of the other squadrons had always covered Barrel Roll in the past, few of us Hobos had ever been up there.

After a while, Rick called on the radio and said he had lost all his navigation equipment. Bill called him back and said not to worry, just stick close.

The clouds were building higher and thicker the further north we went and so were the mountains. In the distance we could make out some of the higher peaks at the southern end of the Himalayas. By the time we neared the target area, the ground below was almost completely obscured by "rock-filled" clouds.

We had tuned our radios to the combat operating frequencies and soon began to pick up all the chatter. It was easy to tell things were pretty tense: everyone's voice was rapid, high pitched, and excited. We found an area of clouds we were pretty sure had a valley beneath. Rick moved into tight formation and after awhile, we broke out (luckily) in the clear. We could see the village of Mong Soui and the base up ahead, and it was covered by even lower clouds and a lot of black smoke.

We checked in with the Raven, who asked us to cover the choppers while they were near the base, and he warned us of the heavy ground fire. We covered them until the choppers had to go back for fuel. After they left, Raven asked us to destroy as much of our munitions and supplies as we could, to prevent them falling into the enemy's hands. Both Bill and Rick were pretty good shots; after two rocket passes, we had blown up so much the smoke obscured what might have been left.

There was a long stack of 55-gallon fuel drums on the north side of the small dirt runway. I suggested that we drop our napalm, unfused, on the drums, let it spread around, and then come back around and hit it with 20-millimeter tracer. That way, we would have a fire rather than an explosion. Bill thought it was a good idea, so we did it. It didn't work too well. Just as we got over the napalm-soaked drums, they ignited. We felt a huge g-load pushing us up into the clouds, and, for a minute, we weren't sure where we were. When we got back down below the clouds, the entire base was so covered with smoke we couldn't see it at all.

While we waited for the smoke to clear, the Raven had another job for us. One of our helicopters had been shot down earlier that morning, and he wanted us to put some 20-millimeter cannon rounds into it and burn it so the bad guys couldn't salvage anything. It's a tribute to the designers of that chopper that we couldn't get the self-sealing fuel tanks to rupture. After a couple of passes the Raven called and said: "Hobos, you are really getting hosed by ground fire from the south!"

Bill rolled back in and started firing at the gun. Their muzzle flash was very clear at that point; suddenly, our right wing (on my side) exploded. Bill broke us off sharply to the right and Rick yelled, "You're hit!" Hell, we already knew that! The fire spread rapidly over the wing, and the skin began to peel off. The 20-millimeter ammunition next to our guns also began exploding. Finally, the right flap broke off. Déjà vu! Based on my own past experience with a wing fire, I knew the wing would start losing lift and we would start one slow, final roll to the right. Sure enough, the roll started, and Bill said, "I can't hold it."

The bailout procedure in the two-seater called for the guy in the right seat (me) to go first. I said I was getting out and then pulled the ejection handle. We surmised later that the canopy failed to fall away as it was supposed to, and the extraction rocket fired through the glass while dragging me with it. In any case, there I was, hanging out in the parachute straps again over some very unfriendly country. I had a chance to look around and see we were about three miles from where all the action had taken place, but I couldn't see Bill's chute or our airplane—not a good sign! Next, I remember thinking, "Why me, again?"

(Author's note: Maj. Bill Bagwell had been forced to bail out on October 2, 1968, less than a year before, from another Douglas A-1E Skyraider, and he was brought down from a gunfire-caused fire in his right wing.)

I looked down; the ground was close and coming up fast. Worse, I headed for the side of a hill where all the trees had been cut down and nothing was left but stumps. How delightful! We had done a lot of parachute landing training in the past; the recommended technique was to land on the balls of our feet, twist slightly, and then land on our hip and shoulder in a rolling motion. I hit toes, crotch, and feet. But I didn't hit a stump!

I got out of the parachute harness and helmet and pulled out my survival radio. The Raven came up right away and said, "Pop a smoke (flare)." Thank God, this time I still had my flares. I tried one and it worked as advertised. About that time I looked around to see if there might be any bad guys around and sure enough, about 200 feet down the hill was a Laotian native coming my way. (Hours later when I was safe and collecting my thoughts in a clear head, I was able to recall this was really a little, very old man in a loincloth without any kind of gun or weapon of any kind.) Still, at that moment, he looked like the Grim Reaper. I took out my pistol and fired a couple of rounds over his head, but he just smiled and kept coming at me.

About then the chopper came on the radio, and the pilot said he had me in his sight but I would have to climb to the top of the hill for the pickup. I was glad to oblige. My legs were like rubber; it was like one of those bad dreams where you struggle and can't quite get away from the dragon. As I neared the top of the hill, the chopper touched down lightly. There was a guy in the door waving me on, but was too smart to get out and help. I finally got to the door, and he yanked me in, just as we lifted off.

Author's Note

Bagwell was taken to Long Thien, which was the main clandestine CIA base in Laos. There he saw Neal and found that Neal's YANKEE seat didn't work at all. Neal just unhooked his harness and the burning, rolling, A-1 aircraft tossed him out. Both men were flown by helicopter to Nakhon Phanom (NKP), which was their home air base in eastern Thailand. Bagwell was taken to a plastic surgeon who was able to treat his forehead, which had a large, loose flap of skin caused by going through the canopy. His knee was badly bruised, requiring many days of medical treatment. The other area of pain was his crotch, which was bruised from the straps of the YANKEE harness. He knew what was causing this soreness, as he had experienced the same problem when bailing out previously using the YANKEE system. Bagwell made a complete recovery from his injuries.

(Raven was the personal call sign of a small group of forward air controllers who were on leave of absence from the Air

Force and attached to the CIA and were headquartered at Long Thien, north of Vientiane, and they flew from various small airstrips around Laos).

The first live extraction test using the Stanley Aviation YANKEE system was conducted on February 16, 1966, with the ejection seat located in the rear cockpit of a North American Aviation T-6 Texan trainer. Test subject Harry W. Schmoll thought the sensation of the extraction process was less violent than the normal opening shock of a parachute. *Stanley Aviation*

This composite photo is of a Stanley Aircraft YANKEE system test at Hurricane Mesa test track in Utah. The ejection sequence begins in the lower left with the tractor rocket pulling the airman (for this test an anthropomorphic dummy) from a simulated aircraft cockpit, and ends the sequence with the airman descending under a completely inflated parachute.
Stanley Aviation

Chapter Eleven

SPECIAL AIRCRAFT EJECTION SEATS

A ircraft with multi-Mach airspeeds capable of altitudes above 50,000 feet required special ejection seats that were designed to protect the aircrews in these environments, and they warrant special attention in any discussion about the history of ejection seats.

NASA/U.S. Air Force/North American Aviation
X-15 Research Aircraft

NAA received a contract to build three X-15 Model NA-240 rocket-powered research aircraft designed to reach altitudes of about 250,000 feet and speeds of 6,600 feet per second (about Mach 6). The extreme aerodynamic heating its structure would experience required a special material called Inconel X (a high-nickel-content steel). The first flight of the X-15 (C/N 240-1, S/N 56-6670) took place on June 8, 1959, from over Edwards Air Force Base in California, and was flown by NAA pilot A. Scott Crossfield.

Three North American Aviation X-15 aircraft were built. The aircraft was designed to reach altitudes of 250,000 feet and a speed of 6,000 feet per second (about Mach 6). The X-15 exceeded those goals and set an absolute speed record of Mach 6.7 and reached an altitude of 354,200 feet. *North American Aviation*

Due to weight and volume restrictions on this research aircraft, NAA wanted to utilize an open-faced ejection with a pressure suit as its escape system. This system was able to work because of two assets at NAA. In the early 1950s, the pilot of the X-15, A. Scott Crossfield, had worked closely with David M. Clark in the development of pressure suits. Crossfield had also flown in the NASA/Douglas D558-2 Skyrocket research aircraft from which that pressure suit had evolved. The Skyrocket utilized an ejectable nose escape system, as did the German Heinkel He-176 and the Bell X-2. While the D558-2 ejectable nose was never used, the X-2's nose was, which resulted in the death of its pilot. Crossfield felt strongly that an ejection seat/pressure-suit combination would provide

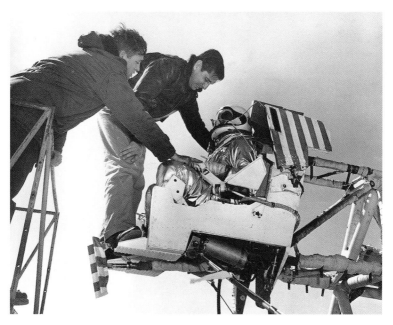

An X-15 ejection seat is being prepared for a high-speed windblast test using a high-speed sled-test track. This is an early version of the seat that was equipped with a shock-wave generator, which appears as the striped device near test pilot Scott Crossfield's feet. *North American Aviation, via Scott Crossfield*

the pilot with the best means of escape. This resulted in the David Clark Co., Scott Crossfield, and a talented NAA designer, Jerry Madden, producing what was at that time the most elaborate ejection seat ever built.

The pressure suit was the key to making this system work. It would protect the pilot from the extremes of the windblast, as an ejecting pilot would enter a multi-Mach airstream. In addition to protecting the pilot from the windblast, the pressure suit also provided the pressurization required at altitudes around 250,000 feet. Even so, it was understood that while the materials from which the pressure suit were built could withstand the temperatures inherent from aerodynamic heating, the pilot would probably receive some blistering in the areas of the helmet, knees, and toes.

A pressure-suited anthropomorphic dummy and an X-15 ejection seat are being subjected to a windblast test at Edwards Air Force Base in California. *North American Aviation*

Let's look at how the NASA/Clark MC-2 pressure suit and ejection seat were integrated into a system to provide a pilot with the maximum protection, while keeping the weight and volume to a minimum. One problem with ejection seats from the beginning has been how to propel a crewman away from the aircraft with sufficient force to clear any of the craft's structure and with sufficient height to allow his parachute to fully inflate in low-altitude situations. On the X-15, a rocket motor–type catapult was used to minimize forces on the spinal column. In addition, a unique method was found for perfect distribution of the load transfer from the seat pan to the man.

Each pilot that was to fly the X-15 sat on a weather balloon filled with plastic beads and wiggled around until it conformed to his derriere. A vacuum was applied to the interior of the balloon, removing the air, which essentially "froze" the pellets into place. After the pilot stepped away, plaster of Paris was poured into the remaining cavity, creating an exact copy of

In this final configuration of the X-15 rocket research aircraft's ejection seat, the shock-wave generator was eliminated and stabilization booms were added. *North American Aviation*

his posterior. A block of balsa wood was then carved to fit the plaster mold. This provided a path that perfectly distributed the ejection loads over the maximum area. This approach also provided two other assets to the X-15: it provided the pilots with a very comfortable seat and, just as important, saved aircraft weight, cost, and complexity. By matching the thickness of the balsa block to that of the pilot's seated height, the seat-height actuator and electrical components were eliminated.

Another problem to be addressed was the flailing of a crewman's arms and legs during ejection, a problem that plagued ejection seats from the beginning. This problem was tackled head-on with the X-15. Prior to ejection, the pilot snapped his legs aft onto the footrests, which closed a pair of shackles to hold his legs place. This operation also raised a pair of deflectors in front of his toes. These deflectors protected his toes from windblast and from aerodynamic heating. Continuing the ejection sequence, the pilot pulled a set of articulated arms up across his body, which began the automatic ejection sequence. This raised a set of thigh restraints, formed elbow and hand restraints, and also provided gauntlets to protect his hands from aerodynamic heating.

Within the last 15 degrees of raising the articulated arms into position, the emergency oxygen supply was activated and the canopy was ballistically removed. This initiated the seat catapult, firing the seat up the ejection rails. Trippers on the rails activated a battery on the seat to keep the pilot's pressure-suit visor clear of ice and activated the aneroid timer.

Wings on the side of the ejection seat folded down to provide stability as the seat moved into the slipstream. It is important to note that the use of a typical fabric drogue chute for this purpose was precluded, as the fabric would have melted in the extreme heat generated by the multi-Mach airflow. As the ejection seat cleared the aircraft, two telescoping booms on the bottom of the seat were extended, providing aerodynamic stability.

This high-speed sled-test qualification was of the final configuration for the eject seat of the X-15 rocket-powered, high-speed research aircraft. *North American Aviation, taken by Bob Schrader*

If ejection took place above 15,000 feet in altitude, the man–seat separation was inhibited, with the pilot remaining in the seat. Due to the prolonged time it could take to free-fall from the extreme altitude the X-15 could attain, two large oxygen bottles were located in the seat pan. As the seat dropped to 15,000 feet, the restraint system was released and the headrest was fired away, deploying the parachute. The opening of the parachute pulled the pilot from his seat for a normal parachute descent. If ejection took place below 15,000 feet, a fixed three-second delay allowed for seat stabilization to take place, prior to the release of the restraint system and parachute deployment effecting man–seat separation.

A little-known fact is that the cockpit of the X-15 was pressurized with nitrogen, with the pilot breathing oxygen from his unpressurized suit. This simplified the X-15's breathing system and created something possibly even more important: a fireproof atmosphere for the cockpit.

The X-15 set an absolute speed record of Mach 6.7 and altitude of 354,200 feet. The ejection seat was never used on the X-15, with two of the aircraft surviving their flight-testing. The third aircraft and its pilot were lost when the ship went out of control and broke up during reentry. Its pilot, Mike Adams, may have been able to survive his X-15 experience if he had ejected during a very small window of time. But the temperatures involved may have precluded that chance for survival. Of the two remaining X-15s, one is on display at The National Air and Space Museum in Washington, D.C., and the other at the Air Force Museum in Dayton, Ohio.

U.S. Government/Lockheed A-12

The A-12 was designed and built under what is called a "black program," as its funding and existence were only known to a few who had a real need to know. The A-12 was designed to cruise in excess of Mach 3 at over 80,000 feet in altitude and was to be utilized as a reconnaissance and attack-strike aircraft. This flight envelope presented many extremely difficult problems to its designers, including finding fuel and hydraulic fluids that would work at such an altitude and within a structure heated to high temperatures due to aerodynamic friction. A second problem was finding a lightweight structural material that could operate with skin temperatures a little over 900 degrees Fahrenheit. The material chosen was titanium, which presented its own problems in forming and corrosion control. A third area of difficulty was designing an engine inlet design that could take the triplesonic airstream and slow it down to the smooth subsonic airflow required at the face of each of the two engines.

The first flight of the Lockheed A-12 (S/N 60-6924) took place on April 26, 1962, from a secret base called Area 51, also known as Groom Lake, which is located in the high desert of Nevada. Lockheed pilot Lou Schalk made the flight. Flight-testing quickly showed that many difficulties were involved in cruising at Mach 3 at these altitudes. As it turned out, the configuration of the engine inlets and control logic took the most time to solve.

To learn how the escape system for the A-12 was chosen, one must step back in time. Stanley Aviation was a builder of ejection seats, many of them being of the downward ejection type. Thus when Lockheed built the XF-104 Starfighter, it chose to use what was termed the Stanley C downward ejection seat. When the F-104 was redesigned to utilize upward ejection

Shown here is a Lockheed A-12 single-place, triplesonic aircraft, the ship from which the SR-71 Blackbird evolved. *Lockheed Martin Skunk Works*

seats, Stanley redesigned their seat into what was called the Stanley C-1, which became a dependable escape system. Later, Lockheed began building the C-1 ejection seat, under license from Stanley. With further refinements, the seat became the C-2 and then later the SR-1, which had an excellent rocket catapult,

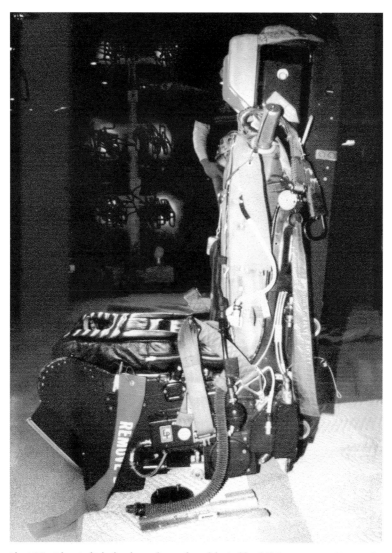

The A-12, triplesonic, high-altitude attack aircraft used this Lockheed SR-1 ejection seat. *Tony Landis*

limb restraint, and a stabilization and retardation system. It was a fully automatic ejection seat. This seat was used in the Lockheed U-2, where weight and space were at a premium and its operating altitude required a pressure suit. So it naturally followed that Lockheed chose to use a proven design on the A-12. Thus, the A-12 pilot was equipped with a U.S. Air Force/David Clark pressure suit and seated in a Lockheed S/R-1 ejection seat.

A-12 Flight-Testing Prologue, by Kenneth S. Collins

The A-12's project pilot selection process took approximately one year to interview and evaluate the physical and mental capabilities for those who would be selected for the OXCART Project. For me, this process began in the last part of 1961. I went to Washington, D.C., for the final indoctrination in October 1962, and reported to my Los Angeles contact in November. In December I was flown to the test site where we would be conducting our flight tests to meet the flight operations staff. Col. Douglas T. Nelson was the director of operations when I reported into the project. This was the first time that there had been any discussions concerning the flying, the name of the aircraft, or the OXCART project. I had not been offered the opportunity to see the aircraft until Colonel Nelson took me to the hangar. This was truly an amazing, breathtaking sight—long, black, low, sleek; the sharp-pointed inlet spikes; the tapered fuselage chines; the oversized engine nacelles with wide canted rudders on top; the double delta wings blending into the fuselage and the fuselage extending way forward of the wings with the pilot's cockpit at the end. It was flat black and looked like a huge swan. Thus the project pilot's own name for this black bird—Cygnus.

The initial four project pilots were Lon Walter, Bill Skliar, Walt Ray, and myself.

SPECIAL AIRCRAFT EJECTION SEATS

On February 4, 1963, Bill Skliar became the first project pilot to fly the A-12 Trainer, which had J-75 engines instead of J-58. The J-58 was having technical problems, so they retrofitted the J-58 nacelles to accommodate the much smaller J-75. It had the same airframe and ejection system. It worked great as a systems trainer; it took off and landed the same, it air-refueled the same. But it could only get out to Mach 1.6.

My first flight was on February 6, 1963. Walt Ray flew on February 10 and Lon Walter a couple of days later. Within a short time after the initial four project pilots reported in, four more pilots had been selected and checked in. They were Mel Vojvodich, Dennis Sullivan, Jack Weeks, and Jack Layton. Frank Murray was brought in from the operations staff. All of the A-12 pilots were the true triplesonic pioneers. The Lockheed test pilots would fly a mission one day and a project pilot would fly the next day or so. We all were "experimental" test pilots. There were six of us selected to be members of the Society of Experimental Test Pilots—Bill Skliar, Mel Vojvodich, Denny Sullivan, Jack Layton, Frank Murray, and myself.

The base had about six F-101 aircraft for the A-12 pilots to fly for general proficiency and instrument training. The F-101 was also used as a "chase" plane for A-12 takeoffs and landings and in case of any other potential A-12 emergency.

The engine and the inlets were the biggest technical problem. There were many other problems, mostly the product of extreme heat at cruise. The engines and the inlets were the greatest hurdle to our getting to 80,000 feet and in excess of Mach 3. Initially, there was not a flight that the inlet didn't un-start, which compressor-stalled the engine(s) and blew out the afterburners. You know the equation: without thrust, you don't fly. If you were passing through 50,000 to 60,000 feet and had an un-start, you were soon down at 15,000 feet after a head-knocking, bone-jarring, uncontrolled plunge. You were attempting to restart the engines, the inlets, and the afterburners all the way down, hoping that you would at least get one engine going. You had 16 shots of TEB (the engine pyrotechnic igniter fluid which required one shot per engine and one for the afterburner) until you could get something going. All this time the cockpit was shaking and vibrating so severely that you could hardly read the instruments and hang onto the throttle and stick. Later someone came up with a more benign term—aerodynamic disturbance—for the inlet un-start. While this type of situation got to be routine for the first year, Pratt & Whitney, the engine people, and Lockheed, who designed the inlet, were working hard to solve this most serious problem.

An A-12 Ejection, by Ken Collins

On May 24, 1963, I was given an A-12 flight to accomplish subsonic engine tests. It was to be a two-hour test flight to check various engine parameters. Jack Weeks, also an A-12 project pilot, was to be my McDonnell Aircraft F-101 Voodoo chase pilot. Normally we suited up in the pressure suit, but this being a subsonic mission, we wore the standard Air Force flight suit. We had an oxygen adapter for our standard flight helmet and oxygen mask in the A-12.

Engine start and takeoff from the secret Groom Lake base were normal and Weeks was close behind in chase position. I was heading north through the Windover Danger Area, which was reserved for OXCART flights. My prebriefed altitude was 24,000 feet. The mission was to fly north to the assigned altitude, about 45 minutes, turn east for about 30 minutes, and then south to return to home base.

After the right turn was completed I began picking up some clouds. Since the chase and I were to maintain safe visual contact, I climbed to 25,000 feet above the denser clouds. The further east we went, the heavier the clouds became. We could not maintain visual flight rules. Weeks, an excellent formation pilot, was sitting on my wing. I made the programmed right turn south, climbing up to 33,000 feet. After completion of the turn, Weeks hand-signaled (during this time of OXCART Project we made no radio transmissions—none. Later, we did have discreet UHF radios in the A-12 and F-101) for me to check my airspeed. I responded that I was on plan. Weeks soon waved that he could no longer stay with me at that airspeed and altitude. I checked all of my instruments and flight situation. Everything was reading normal. Weeks said he could not stay with me. I told him to head back and that I would see him at home.

I began to realize that while the flight instruments were indicating correctly, the feel of the aircraft was not right. I engaged the autopilot to check out its response, but that didn't help either. I even took off my leather flight gloves in an attempt to get a finer feel of the controls. I caught the altimeter beginning to show an ever-increasing descent—unwinding—and at the same time the airspeed indicator was showing a rapid decrease. The attitude indicator was indicating I was level. At this point, seeing the instruments were going wild, I could not rely on my altitude or airspeed. The altimeter continued its rapid decrease, as did the airspeed. I saw the 102 knots indicated airspeed and the A-12 did pitch-up and go inverted into a flat insipid, an unrecoverable spin. I cycled the control stick left, right, forward, aft, with zero response. I was upside down in the weather with no means of determining my exact altitude. I knew that I was over mountainous terrain, but I did not how high I was above the mountains.

I knew that the only way to get out of the situation was to eject from the A-12. I also knew that the rocket jet ejection seat system could push you up into a 300-foot trajectory with zero elevation and zero speed. I had minimum time to consider, because I was ejecting downward.

I reached between my legs, grabbed the D-ring, pushed my head firmly back into the headrest and pulled the D-ring and ejected. The canopy and I, in the seat, cleared the aircraft immediately. The man-separator did its job by pushing me away from the heavy ejection seat. Following the seat-separation sequence, my parachute automatically deployed. I felt the tug from the harness; I looked up and confirmed the canopy was there, a very comforting feeling. I looked down to survey the terrain on which I would have to land and recover. I instantly went from a secure feeling to a state of absolute fear—the parachute had separated and I was free-falling. I knew that my luck had run out and that I would quickly hit the ground in a matter of moments. But in a matter of seconds my whole body came to a stop, almost as if I were rising up. The main chute had opened and my rate of descent had been reduced. The initial chute deployment was the drogue chute, which was programmed to deploy after seat separation and to separate when dropping through 15,000 feet. There is a three-second delay from drogue chute separation and the main chute deploying and opening. To me, it seemed like an eternity!

I assumed the parachute fall position, hit the desert floor, and rolled onto my left shoulder. I immediately hit the riser releases and spilled the canopy. Confirming that I had no injuries except the bruised shoulder, I began gathering the parachute canopy for survival. I also picked up some of the pages of my flight checklist, which were classified.

As I was mentally preparing myself for a camp out, I was pleasantly surprised by the bounding approach of a pickup truck coming across the rough desert. They had retrieved the aircraft canopy, which was in the bed of their truck. I threw my gear in the back and squeezed in the cab with them and asked to be taken to the nearest highway patrol office, and we arrived there in about 30 minutes. I made one telephone call and in two or three hours, two aircraft landed at Wendover Airfield, one with security and maintenance personnel and the other to take me to the Lovelace Clinic for a physical checkup.

The ejection system had worked as advertised and I was fine. An engineer eventually discovered the primary cause of the system failures: the pitot/static tube had inadequate heating, allowing ice to form and give false airspeed and altitude readings. As if that wasn't enough, I had experienced a failure in the air data computer. As Kelly Johnson had said, the whole A-12 aircraft had to be reinvented. The Rosemont Probe, a new pitot/static tube, was one of those inventions.

An A-12 Ejection, Part II, by Mel Vojvodich

Here it was, December 28, 1968, and I asked myself, "Why aren't I home with my family enjoying the Christmas holiday, rather than out here at a remote Nevada desert secret air base called Area 51?" Because I was a project pilot on what was known as the OXCART Project.

I was to fly a Lockheed A-12, which certainly wasn't a clunker, on a test flight after a major modification. The aircraft was a single-seater, so this would be a solo flight. Along with the Lockheed crew chief, I carefully did a preflight walkaround, then entered the cockpit, fastened my harness, made sure all my personal leads were connected, and began the preengine start checklist. As this was a check flight, I would not fly at the extreme speed and altitude limits of this high-performance aircraft. So instead of a pressure suit I was in the standard flight suit and helmet. Everything checked out okay, so I proceeded to start both engines, with all the engine needles within limits.

All systems were go and so I taxied to the end of the active runway for a final run-up. After both afterburners lit off, I released the brakes, accelerated down the runway, rotating at 170 knots, and was airborne at about 200 knots. Almost instantly I got a severe right yaw (the aircraft slewed to the right). I countered with rudder and the aircraft went into a wild pitch-up. The airplane and I went through several events, and finally I decided the only way out was to eject. At the time, I was only at about 200 feet in altitude and in an uncommanded bank of about 40 degrees with the aircraft nose pitching down.

I never felt the parachute-opening shock. I tried to disconnect my survival pack, but hit the dry lakebed before I could get it clear. I hit the lakebed in an extremely poor attitude and almost ended up in the fireball of my crashed A-12! I hit so hard that I was temporarily paralyzed from the waist down. I used my arms to drag myself clear of the fire. Mercifully, the fire trucks and paramedics arrived in about five minutes.

After a checkup it was found that I only received minor bruises, thanks to the performance of one fine Lockheed ejection seat equipped with its rocket motor. These flights were being filmed by ground-mounted cameras and after development confirmed that I was at about 200 feet in altitude when I ejected. These films also showed that if I had been in a two-seat-type aircraft, one of us would not have survived. The subsequent accident investigation showed that a technician had cross-wired the stability augmentation system. The result was that when I pulled back on the stick, I got yaw, and when I corrected yaw with rudder, I got pitch up or down.

U.S. Air Force/Lockheed SR-71 Blackbird

The two-place Lockheed SR-71 Blackbird evolved from the single-place Lockheed A-12 and its primary mission was reconnaissance. The first flight of the SR-12 (S/N 64-17951) was made on December 22, 1964, from Palmdale Airport, in Palmdale, California. The pilot was Lockheed test pilot Robert Gilliland.

The choice of the escape system to be used in the Blackbird was fairly simple: make a slight upgrade from the ejection seat utilized by the A-12, which flew in the same general altitude and speed range. This seat had been improved, step by step,

Shown here is a Lockheed two-place, high-altitude SR-71 Blackbird reconnaissance aircraft. The Blackbird evolved from the Lockheed A-12. *Lockheed Martin Skunk Works*

beginning with the Stanley Aviation downward ejection seat used on the Lockheed F-104. Later, the seat was redesigned to become an upward ejection seat used in the F-104. Then the seat was used in the Lockheed U-2. With more improvements, it was used in the A-12, and then it became the dependable Lockheed-built escape system for the SR-71.

Escape from a Disabled SR-71

On January 25, 1966, Lockheed test pilot William A. Weaver and Lockheed Reconnaissance Systems Operator James Zwayer were at about 80,000 feet in altitude in their U.S. Air Force/Lockheed SR-71 Blackbird with a speed of over

The Lockheed Aircraft SR-2 ejection seat was designed for the SR-71 Blackbird triplesonic, high-altitude reconnaissance aircraft. *Tony Landis*

Mach 3 and in a 30-degree right-bank turn when they experienced an un-start condition in the right engine inlet. An inlet un-start is a violent condition that not only eliminates the thrust of the engine being fed air by the un-started inlet, but also adds tremendous aerodynamic drag to that side of the aircraft. The combination of an abnormal aft center of gravity, the aircraft being in a banked condition, the loss of thrust on their right engine, and high drag forces, caused the aircraft to enter a yawed, pitch-up condition.

Weaver was attempting to recover from this unstable flight condition, but the aerodynamic forces required exceeded the restoring capability of the flight controls. Within seconds it became obvious to Weaver that the situation was hopeless. He called Zwayer on the intercom and asked him to try to stay with the aircraft until they were at a lower speed and altitude. At their present altitude and airspeed, Weaver didn't think ejection would be successful. The men were being subjected to incredibly high g-forces. Within seconds, the forces being experienced exceeded the aircraft's structural limits. Dutch 64 broke up, with the forward fuselage separating from the rest of the aircraft, causing Weaver to black out.

The remainder of the story is told in Weaver's own words:

I thought I was having a bad dream and hoped that I would wake up and this would go away. However, as I began to regain consciousness, I realized it was not a dream and this really had happened. At that point, I thought I was dead because I was convinced that I could not have survived what had happened. I remember thinking that being dead wasn't so bad after all—I had kind of a detached, euphoric feeling. As I became more conscious, I realized I wasn't dead after all, and that I somehow became separated from the aircraft. I couldn't see anything as my face mask had iced up.

My pressure suit had inflated, so I knew the emergency oxygen supply in the seat kit was functioning. This provided not only breathing oxygen and pressurization essential at those altitudes, but also physical protection against the intense buffeting and g-forces to which I had been subjected. It was like being in your own life-support capsule. After realizing that I wasn't dead and that I was free of the aircraft, I was concerned about stability and not tumbling at such high altitude. Centrifugal forces sufficient to cause physical damage can be generated if the body tumbles at high altitude where there is little air density to resist these motions. Fortunately, the small stabilization chute designed to prevent tumbling had worked just fine.

My next concern was the main chute: would the barometric automatic opening device work at 15,000 feet? I certainly hadn't made a proper exit—I knew I had not initiated the ejection procedure. How long had I been blacked out and how high was I? I was about to open my the faceplate so that I could see and try to estimate my altitude and locate my parachute D-ring, when I felt a sharp, reassuring tug, which indicated that the main chute had deployed. I managed to raise the faceplate and visibility was just incredible. It was a clear winter day, about three in the afternoon, and from my vantage point beneath the parachute canopy it appeared that I could see for a couple hundred miles. But what made everything just perfect was that about one-quarter mile away was Jim's chute. I was delighted, because I didn't believe either of us could have survived, and to think that Jim had also made it gave me an incredible lift.

I couldn't manipulate the risers to steer my chute because my hands were frozen and I needed one hand just to keep the iced-up visor raised (the latch was broken). As a result, I could only see in one direction and the terrain wasn't all that inviting. I was convinced we'd have to spend at least the night out there, and I was trying to think of things I had been taught in survival training. I landed okay and was trying to undo my parachute harness when I heard a voice say, "Can I help you?" I looked up and there was a guy walking towards me wearing a cowboy hat and behind him was a helicopter. He turned out to be Albert Mitchell Jr. and, as I learned later, he owned the huge cattle ranch in northeast New Mexico upon which I had landed. He helped me out of the chute, told me he had radioed the police, Air Force, and the nearest hospital and then said, "I saw your buddy coming down; I'll go and help him."

He climbed into his helicopter and was back a few minutes later with the devastating news that Jim was dead. I asked him to take me over to Jim, and after verifying that there was nothing that could be done, he flew me to Tucumcari hospital about 60 miles to the south. I have vivid memories of that flight, as well. Being a pilot, I knew about redlines, and the airspeed needle was at or above the redline all the way to Tucumcari. I thought about the possibility of that little craft shaking itself apart in flight. How ironic it would be to have miraculously survived the previous disaster only to be finished off in the helicopter that had come to my rescue! We made it without mishap, and upon reaching the hospital I was able to phone Lockheed Flight Test at Edwards Air Force Base in California. They knew the aircraft had been lost and couldn't believe that I had survived.

Author's Note

Upon subsequent investigation, they found both ejection seats in the wreckage of the forward fuselage. It is supposed that during the breakup of the aircraft both canopies were torn off. Then a combination of g-forces and air loads caused both men to be thrown out of the aircraft. It was at this point that the automatic features of their escape systems took over. It was probably at this point that the neck of Jim Zwyer was broken, resulting in his death.

After Weaver described what had occurred after the engine un-start, engineers at Lockheed were able to duplicate the situation on the SR-71 flight simulator with the same results. The main preventive measure was not to intentionally exceed aft center of gravity limit on subsequent flights. The inlet control system was eventually redesigned and became much more reliable.

It turned out that Weaver's hands were not frozen, but only numb from the extreme low temperatures he had experienced when thrown from the Blackbird. Normal functions returned to his hands once they warmed. Weaver and his family visited Mitchell's ranch the summer following the accident. Once again he flew with Mitchell in what he found out was a Hughes helicopter, only this time under more pleasant circumstances. Weaver found out that at the time of the accident, Mitchell was branding colts in a corral near a hanger where he kept his helicopter. Mitchell heard a loud boom and saw strange-looking vapor trails in the sky. As he continued to watch these trails, he spotted two parachutes, fired up his helicopter, and flew the two miles to where Weaver had landed. He arrived at about the same time that Weaver touched down.

Shown here is an SR-71 slow-speed ejection seat test with an aircraft nose section being towed across the desert. As a "black" program, the SR-71 was under extreme security limits. Thus, this unique form of testing was chosen over the sled-test track at Edwards Air Force Base in California. *Tony Landis*

Chapter Twelve

Supersonic Fighter Challenges

With the advent of the Century fighters, all at once U.S. aircraft were capable of supersonic flight. Yet these aircraft were still fitted with ejection seats that weren't designed to safely eject into a supersonic airstream.

U.S. Air Force/NAA F-100 Super Sabre Fighter

NAA Model 180, YF-100A Super Sabre (C/N 180-1, S/N 52-5754) was first flown on May 25, 1953, from Edwards Air Force Base in California by George S. "Wheaties" Welch. This was a unique first flight, as he took this untested ship supersonically on its first flight. The F-100 entered production as a single-place fighter, as a two-place fighter-bomber, and as a two-place trainer, with almost 2,300 built. The escape system was a NAA-designed ejection seat that had evolved from the manual system of the early F-86 Sabres to a completely automatic system.

The North American F-100 Super Sabre fighter flew supersonic on its maiden flight. *Boeing Historical Archives*

The World's First Successful Supersonic Ejection

George Smith was a production test pilot for NAA. On Saturday, February 26, 1955, his day off from work, he stopped by work to drop off a report. His boss prevailed upon him to fly chase on two NAA F-100 Super Sabre fighters that were taxiing for takeoff. Smith agreed, only having time to don his parachute, Mae West, and helmet over his street clothes.

As he was taxiing out in his F-100A, he noticed the flight-control stick bind, or stiffen, in the pitch axis. He thought the artificial-feel system was acting up. Then the stick became free and he continued on to take off from the Los Angeles International Airport runway. He had started his turn out over the Pacific Ocean when the stickiness returned. He was considering calling the tower and returning to base, when the problem cleared itself. He continued on to catch up with the other two aircraft. At about an altitude of 35,000 feet over Laguna Beach he saw the contrails of the other ships, when suddenly the F-100 pitched over into a near vertical dive. Smith attempted to overpower the stick and get the nose up, but to no avail. He used pitch trim, but as the speed increased to Mach 1 the nose tucked under and steepened the dive even more. Smith had radioed his problem, and the NAA tower and the other F-100s yelled for him to eject.

Shown here is an ejection seat used on the F-100 Super Sabre. This is the same model that was used by North American Aviation production test pilot George Smith and U.S. Air Force 1st Lt. Russ Scott to eject from their ailing fighters. *North American Aviation*

EJECT!

Since he could not regain control, Smith pulled the ejection handles as he passed through 6,000 feet at a speed of Mach 1.05. The canopy was ripped off into the supersonic slipstream. A thunderous clap filled Smith's head as the shock wave filled the cockpit as he pulled the ejection triggers. He lost consciousness as the ejection seat moved out into the slipstream. The helmet was ripped from his head, his eyes were severely mauled, his nose was literally torn from his upper lip, and his internal body filled like a balloon from the air pressure. His shoes, watch ring, dye-marker, and flashlight were torn from his body, and his clothes were shredded. The aneroid device on his parachute activated his ripcord, and as the parachute canopy was pulled out, the vicious airstream immediately tore out several parachute panels. The descent rate of the unconscious pilot was much higher than normal. The other two F-100s caught up with Smith and saw him dropping like a rock under his damaged chute.

Meanwhile, a small boat was directly under Smith, about a thousand yards off Dana Point, when the crippled F-100 dove directly into the wake of their boat, lifting it clear out of the water and killing both of its engines. The three fellows in the boat thought they were being bombed or shelled and started the boat to get out of there fast. They then saw Smith, first thinking he was a dummy dropped from the same plane that had bombed them but then realizing when they saw blood dripping from Smith's feet as he dropped into the water that it was a real person. Smith was so bloated from the internal air that he bobbed back to the surface, floating chest-high out of the water. Even though they could only get one of their boat engines started, they got to Smith and cut him out of his harness and pulled him onboard. As the boat limped back toward Newport Beach, they waved down a large cabin cruiser that picked up Smith and carried him at high speed.

Smith was in a coma for six days and couldn't see for a month. He suffered liver and kidney damage and had to have his gall bladder removed, as well as about 17 feet of his intestines. Every joint in his arms and legs had been dislocated. Yet he had survived the first open-seat supersonic ejection in history.

About a year later Smith was back flying F-100s and with the help of a hypnotist, he was able to remember this flight. The shattered F-100 was salvaged from the ocean and the probable cause was a blocked hydraulic valve in the tail section. The fix was to double the hydraulic return lines and also to add hydraulic fuses. With a fuse (a thin metal diaphragm), a pilot could overpower a similar blockage by bursting the fuse open by inputting sufficient force on his flight-control stick.

A Slow-Speed Bailout from an F-100

U.S. Air Force 1st Lt. Russell Scott was part of the Second Tactical Fighter Wing located at Royal Air Force Station Wethersfield in England. At that time, North American was installing field kits on the F-100Ds in Chalon Vatry, France. This kit was to provide a backup system for the aircraft's wheel brakes. After the kits were installed, each ship was taken for a functional check flight prior to being returned to its unit.

Scott was qualified to perform these functional check flights, and on February 10, 1958, he arrived at Chalon Vatry to take one of these modified F-100Ds up for its check flight. The check flight required that a number of functional checks be performed as stated on a detailed test card. Scott was at 30,000 feet in altitude and had reached the step to where, by the use of a cockpit switch, he would simulate the loss of hydraulic system pressure. This action was to automatically open a door on the topside of the fuselage to allow engine inlet air to flow through the ram air turbine (RAT). The purpose of the turbine

Shown here is a sled test of North American Aviation's ejection seat for a two-place F-100 Super Sabre fighter. Note that the forward seat has just cleared the cockpit as the aft seat's rocket motor has already burned out and the man–seat separation has begun. *North American Aviation*

was to generate sufficient hydraulic pressure to the flight controls to get a plane safely down to land in the event the engine-driven hydraulic pumps failed.

Almost as soon as the RAT door was opened, Scott heard a loud bang, which indicated he had experienced an engine compressor stall. As the engine rpm began winding down, Scott pushed the nose of the F-100 down to effect the best glide angle and attempted to restart the engine. He made several unsuccessful restart attempts, hoping that at a lower altitude he could get enough engine thrust to allow him to limp back to base.

Below him were several villages and he delayed ejection to clear them, still hoping to get the engine to start. This was not to be, and at 2,000 feet and at about 220 knots he knew he had to leave the stricken aircraft. Scott pulled up on the ejection seat handles, which fired the canopy off, and then he pulled the seat triggers to begin the automatic ejection sequence.

Just clear of the aircraft Scott was amazed as he began tumbling violently. Even though he had his oxygen mask attached, his visor locked down, and his helmet chinstrap fastened, they were immediately stripped off his head. Next, he heard a loud popping noise and looked up to see a most beautiful sight: a fully inflated canopy on his parachute. He landed in a plowed field and, other than some bruising, came through the ejection unhurt. The F-100, having been trimmed at 220 knots and wings level, made a perfect belly landing in a wheatfield. It shed both wings during the slide; before coming to a halt, the engine broke loose and exited the aircraft through the cockpit. This proved a good example of why not to attempt a belly landing in a high-performance aircraft.

Within a day or so, Scott was back to flying F-100s. He later found that the wild tumbling he experienced was typical for that ejection seat at that speed and altitude. A postcrash investigation revealed that the blades of the RAT had failed during spin-up and had gone through the engine compressor, which caused a very bad case of foreign object damage.

Chapter Thirteen

ENCAPSULATED EJECTION SEATS

Encapsulated ejection seats provided flight crews with several benefits that open ejection seats did not. The use of encapsulated seats eliminated the use of pressure suits for high-altitude flights. Encapsulated seats also provided windblast protection if ejection occurred at high speeds. Finally, this type of seat provided post-ejection shelter on the ground or in the sea.

U.S. Air Force/Convair B-58 Hustler Bomber

The Convair B-58 was a three-place supersonic bomber. The first flown was an XB-58 (S/N/55-0660) with its maiden flight on November 11, 1956, from Carswell Air Force Base in Texas. The pilot was Beryl A. Ericson, assisted by J. D. McEachern as copilot and C. P. Harrison as flight-test engineer. Thirty preproduction YB-58 models were built, plus 86 production B-58As. The first 15 aircraft were equipped with state-of-the-art Convair ejection seats, built mostly of magnesium. These seats included head and limb restraint and yet could not cope with the tremendous windblast associated with ejecting into a Mach 2 airstream.

For this reason Stanley Aviation was chosen to design and develop an encapsulated seat for each of the three crew members. In addition to the encapsulated seat being a means of escape from this high-performance aircraft, the encapsulated seat would give the crew two other important features.

The Convair three-place, four-engine, doublesonic B-58 Hustler carried its bomb load externally. It also had encapsulated ejection seats. *Convair, via Lockheed Martin*

The first feature was that the crew would now fly in what was termed a shirtsleeve environment, which meant the crew would no longer be required to wear partial-pressure suits. In the event of the loss of cockpit pressurization, each crew member could close his capsule doors to form an airtight enclosure pressurized to the equivalent of 37,500 feet in altitude. The pilot's encapsulated seat differed from the other two in that it had a larger window and contained the flight-control stick that allowed him to maintain control of the airplane. In addition, his capsule contained switches to control the aircraft's center of gravity and to retard the throttles. Thus, in the event of a loss of cabin pressurization, he could fly the aircraft down to an altitude to where the three crew members could open their capsule doors.

Looking down into the three-crew stations of the Convair Hustler, the upper surface of the three Stanley Aviation encapsulated ejection seats can be seen with the open hatches. *Convair, via Lockheed Martin*

ENCAPSULATED EJECTION SEATS

The second advantage to the encapsulated seat was that in the event of ejection, each crew member would be provided with his own survival shelter. The shelter would protect the crew members from heat or cold or winds and also act as a life raft if landing occurred in water. Stored within the capsule were food, water, a survival radio, and survival gear, including matches, fishing gear, a signaling mirror, flares, and other equipment.

Because the installation of an encapsulated seat would be retrofitted into an existing design that was well into production, the engineers at Stanley had to fit their encapsulated seat within the same space envelope as the open-face ejection seat. This not only impacted the design envelope of the encapsulated seat but also impacted the equipment located within.

How It Works

To understand the complex problem of getting a crew member from the cabin of the B-58 to a safe landing, let's go through the steps involved. To begin the ejection sequence, the crew member pulls up either or both ejection handles—one on each side of the capsule seat. Raising the handles fires a gas generator, which retracts the torso-retracting inertia reel and the leg-positioning mechanism. The body restraints draw the occupant back against the seat with his head against the headrest. His legs are raised by the forward part of the seat pan and a bar beneath his thighs near his knees. Cushioned bars then draw his feet back into the capsule.

When the leg-positioning thrusters have completed their stroke, gas pressure is routed to the door-uplock release and the door-closure thruster. This releases the doors and rotates them downward to form the pressure-tight compartment around the occupant. As the doors close, the capsule pressurization system is activated to an altitude equivalent of 37,500 feet. The doors close and lock within 1/2 to 1 second after the

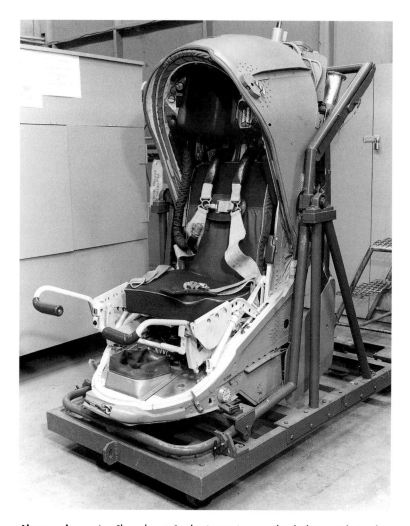

Above and opposite: Shown here is Stanley Aviation's encapsulated pilot's seat designed for the Convair B-58 Hustler bomber. The capsule's windows provided visual access to the instruments. *Convair, via Lockheed Martin*

ejection handle is raised. An additional 5 to 7 seconds may be required for pressurization at high altitude.

The crew member squeezes either one of his ejection triggers in the ejection handles. The first part of the travel fires the canopy actuator to jettison the canopy, and the last part of

travel fires the rocket catapult initiator. The initiator has a 0.3-second time delay to ensure adequate time for canopy removal. In the event the canopy fails to jettison, the encapsulated seat will push off the canopy.

As the capsule travels up the ejection rails, a trip-lever ballistically deploys a stabilization frame and parachute. If ejection is initiated above 15,000 feet, the recovery parachute is inhibited until reaching 15,000 feet. Upon deployment, the

EJECT!

1 CANOPY JETTISONED, CATAPULT FIRES

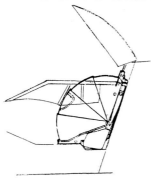

2 FULL EMERGENCE, STABILIZATION CHUTE DEPLOYED

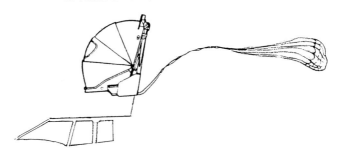

3 RECOVERY CHUTE DEPLOYED

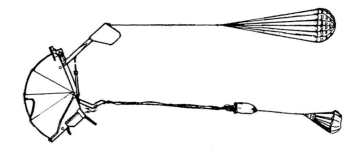

ENCAPSULATED EJECTION SEATS

6 WATER LANDING

5 GROUND LANDING

4 CAPSULE DESCENT

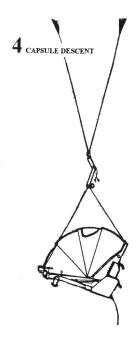

Shown here is the encapsulated seat sequence
during ejection for a Convair B-58 Hustler
doublesonic bomber. *Convair, via Lockheed Martin*

recovery parachute is held in a reefed condition for two seconds to minimize opening shock. The recovery parachute was a 41-foot-diameter ring-sail, which reduced the capsule's rate of descent to a maximum of 28 feet per second. Crushable cylinders on the back of the capsule and the stabilization fins cutting through metal flanges absorbed the ground impact.

Upon deployment of the recovery parachute, the stabilization frame retracts and four telescoping floatation booms are extended by high-pressure gas from ballistic devices. If ejection is begun at or below 15,000 feet, the final descent altitude of the capsule is reached within 10 seconds after the ejection trigger is squeezed.

The Stanley Aviation encapsulated seat had a safe ejection envelope of 100 knots at zero altitude to the maximum operational flight envelope of the Hustler. If the capsule lands in water, its occupant can inflate the flotation bags on the upper booms from a pressurization container. A hand-operated pump is provided for inflating the flotation bags on the other two flotation booms. The control handle for inflating the upper flotation bags also releases the recovery parachute. Almost 57 pounds of survival equipment was stored within the capsule.

Each of the three encapsulated seats worked independently of the other. Assuming the aircraft was stable and time was available, a back-to-front ejection sequence was recommended to minimize the chance of the capsules hitting each other. Each capsule weighed 494 pounds and flight-testing was done with anthropomorphic dummies as well as live and animal subjects.

Early in 1961, a static test was conducted in Fort Worth, Texas, with a dummy in the capsule. The capsule was ejected from the middle cockpit of the B-58 Hustler, ship number two, which was parked. The test showed that at zero airspeed the encapsulated seat components had insufficient time for the recovery parachute to fully inflate and retard the seat to a safe impact rate. The test was repeated using the same aircraft in

Shown here is test subject and U.S. Air Force Sgt. Bill Barber on a Stanley Aviation encapsulated seat that had just completed its 24-hour ocean survival test. *Convair, via Lockheed Martin*

October 1961, but this time at Edwards Air Force Base in California. This time the aircraft was accelerated to a speed of 155 miles per hour and, while still on the runway, the seat was manually ejected. The capsule attained a height of about 250 feet and with both the drogue and recovery parachutes operating correctly, the capsule landed 1,500 feet down the runway and 15 feet off to the side. The test was a success.

The first test with a human subject was conducted at an airspeed of 565 miles per hour (Mach 0.8) from 20,000 feet in altitude. The subject was CWO Edward J. Murray, and this was his 850th parachute jump, including one he made over France on D-Day. As a safety precaution, Murray wore his own parachute, in case the capsule parachute didn't function. In that event he could override the capsule system, open the doors, and bail out in a normal manner. This was not needed, as the test was quite successful and upon landing, Murray said, "No sweat!" Additional testing with bears and chimpanzees was done. The highest-speed ejection was at Mach 2.0 at 47,000 feet on August 21, 1962, also conducted using a B-58 mother ship.

Judging by its outward appearance, this Convair ejection seat, used by U.S. Air Force Capt. Monty Montgomery to bail out of his ailing B-58 Hustler bomber, seems undamaged after its free fall to earth. *Monty Montgomery*

Ejecting from an Early Ejection Seat-Equipped YB/RB-58A Hustler, by Kenneth G. Timpson

I left the U.S. Air Force in 1956 after going through Aviation Cadets, completing a tour in Korea, flying the Lockheed F-80 Shooting Star with the 45th Tactical Recon Squadron, and then flying as an instructor pilot at Williams Air Force Base in Arizona. I then left the U.S. Air Force to complete my studies at Michigan State College and obtain a bachelor of science degree in engineering.

While in college, I joined the Michigan Air National Guard and flew the Northrop F-89 Scorpion. After graduating, I joined the Convair Aircraft Company as a flight-test engineer on the B-58 Hustler program. Who could resist that airplane? It was astounding—it looked like it was going 600 knots just sitting there on its landing gear. The airplane assigned to the second program with which I became involved was YB/RB-58 serial No. 58-1023 (the 30th off the production line, called "Number 30"). Even though this was the first production-standard Hustler, it was fitted with Convair ejection seats instead of the planned Stanley encapsulated seats.

This ship had been taken for its maiden flight on July 24, 1959. Walt Simon and I were the flight-test engineers assigned and had the responsibility to plan and conduct the flight-testing required to develop the navigation-bombing system and to demonstrate that it met the Air Force specifications for the system.

Ray Tenhoff was the pilot assigned to the program. We three flew the test flights—Ray in the first station, Walt in the second, and I in the third. Ray flew the beast, Walt ran the systems, and I ran the instrumentation and the data recording system and performed the airplane flight engineer tasks (fuel distribution, flight performance calculations, and helping the pilot use airplane subsystems).

Flight number 40 was planned to go from Carswell Air Force Base in Texas to the Great Salt Lake, then make two test runs up and down the lake and return to Ft. Worth. The primary purpose of the plan was to obtain data regarding the operation of the Doppler radar over a large body of water that was smooth with no waves, and the Great Salt Lake was a perfect test site for the objective. We took off at about 1:00 P.M. on April 22, 1960, and headed out towards Amarillo and then on to Salt Lake. We had the big pod on and weighed about 146,000 pounds at takeoff. After passing Amarillo we had to climb to 38,000 feet to maintain visual flight rule conditions. But that was not a problem with the four J-79 jets (four Pratt & Whitney turbojet engines) at minimum afterburner for the climb. We cruised at 0.92 Mach at 38,000 feet on up to the Great Salt Lake, doing navigation work, and radar-scored bomb runs. We made the two Doppler runs over the lake (one north and one south) and then discussed repeating the runs because we were having difficulty maintaining a good line over the lake due to poor air-ground visibility. So far this test flight had been rather routine, and although system operation was not too good, we were getting the data to find out why. Repeating the Doppler runs would take about 30 minutes, and we had plenty of fuel and the decision was made to get some more data over the lake.

It was during the turn from north to south that the incident occurred. Walt said something like, "Hey, what are you doing?" or "What is the matter?" and Ray replied, "I don't know." I looked out my right window and observed a nose-high attitude. It did not look severe or startling and then the airplane rolled slowly to the right as if controlled by the pilot. It appeared very much like the procedure used to recover from a nose-high attitude in a T-33. Then a rapid, but not abrupt, yaw to the left occurred and the wings came to almost level. It was at about this time that I thought a bailout could become necessary, and I shoved the paperwork and clipboard off my lap, positioned myself for ejection, put on my oxygen mask, turned the oxygen on, and pulled my visor down. It was very soon after this that I saw that we were in a spin to the left with the airspeed varying between 0 and 120 knots. My altimeter was unwinding faster than I had ever seen before, and I began calling out altitude at about 28,000 feet. The flight conditions were very benign—smooth, quiet, lights on.

At about 17,000 feet I heard "Go!" I said "Three going," and immediately pulled both handgrips up. As the canopy left the airplane the daylight looked hazy, like heat waves off of concrete on hot days. I don't remember any explosive decompression, and there was no debris flying around or buffeting in the crew compartment. I squeezed both triggers and saw the instrument panel leave me. I then remember tumbling head-over-heels forward through the air and having a desperate desire to hang on to the seat. After a few revolutions it occurred to me that if I did not separate from the seat, the parachute would not deploy, so I let go of the handles and the seat left me.

The chute immediately opened—nicely and with very little shock. I looked down and left and saw a series of concentric circles in the water. The diameter was very large and I supposed that the airplane hitting the water caused the circle. I looked for the other two parachutes but didn't see any, but they would have been above me and my parachute was blocking my view upward. I released the raft and survival kit and saw that they were dangling on the tether, attached to the chute as designed. The waves started getting more defined and then, bang, I was in the water.

I am a decent swimmer but was having a problem with my clothes, heavy boots, helmet, and I swallowed a lot of salt water. My feet kept sinking and I tried harder to swim to the raft. Then my feet touched bottom and I stood up waist deep in water about 3/4 of a mile from shore. I pulled the raft to me and leaned on it, feeling a little sick from the saltwater.

I looked for the other two guys, but I couldn't see them and I had no response when I yelled their names. I climbed into the raft and started paddling with my hands to help the light wind, which was pulling the parachute and me toward shore. But I didn't seem to be moving. I pulled the sea anchor in and discovered the survival kit was resting on the bottom, acting like an anchor. So I pulled the kit up and tried to swing it into the boat—earning two punctures in the raft that I could barely plug with my thumb and little finger. I detached from the parachute, climbed out of the boat, threw the kit into the boat, and proceeded to wade to shore, pushing and pulling the boat.

The time was about 1630 with overcast skies, and I think that the temperature was in the 60s. I unzipped the waterproof rucksack that contained the very neatly packed survival gear and found that all the stuff was wet! I removed everything and dumped the water out. After reading the instructions for the radio, I began broadcasting, "Mayday, Mayday, this is a Mayday. Does anyone read?" No one answered. I checked the radio attachments and noticed that the battery was warm and the connector was bubbling. I disconnected everything and tried to dry the connections and after reassembly, tried again. No answers. I tried a few more times later in the day with no response. I then fired my rifle in three-shot patterns a few times, but no response to that either. I now understood that I would be on this beach for at least the night and should prepare for a cool night.

I decided that I should get some logs for wind protection and for a fire and stay on the beach in hopes that someone was looking for us and would see the fire. I found a place with lots of dry wood and a spot where there was a shelf about 2 feet high that would protect me from a north wind. I found some logs to build up the shelf a little higher and to put on the sides, forming a little open-topped cave.

I then gathered enough firewood for a week's stay and got the fire going—my matches worked!! All this movement had pretty well dried my clothes and even though I was covered with salt, I was not injured. I had a fire going and was relatively comfortable. I made the decision during the night to head south in the morning.

At dawn, I packed all of my gear except the radio and oxygen mask, put on my helmet, and started walking south. Approximately two hours later I saw a ramshackle barn and what looked like a two-wheeled house trailer. I yelled "Hello" many times but no one came out. Then I saw the door open and the muzzle of a rifle pointing at me. My appearance was probably quite startling to a person isolated in the wilderness of Utah: my orange flight suit covered with salt, a hard-hat liner on my head, a hard hat in one hand, a rucksack on my back, and a rifle in my other hand. Needless to say, I dropped everything and raised my hands above my head. The person behind the door was a Basque sheepherder: Cris Chulos was his name. He opened the door and told me to come in (he kept his carbine in his hand). I explained my situation to him carefully and thoughtfully and evidently convinced him that I was not a threat, and he put the gun down. He fed me breakfast—ham and eggs (liberally sprinkled with salt and pepper), coffee, and water. Every bit was great and delicious. I asked him for a telephone and he told me there was one six miles south. I asked if he would loan me a horse and he said "No." I asked if he would sell me a horse and he said "No." He needed his horses to handle his sheep, and I was perfectly capable of walking six miles. He was a pragmatic man and was absolutely right in his decision for the utilization of the available assets to do his and my jobs.

So I resumed my walk south with all of my gear. At midday I passed through a deserted construction camp. At least I thought it was deserted—no one answered my calls and there was no smoke coming out of chimneys. About an hour later I heard a helicopter and immediately got the smoke flares out of my rucksack and reread the instructions. I saw a chopper, but the chopper did not see me. I arrived at the railroad in the late afternoon, where there were quite a few buildings and a few trucks. I yelled every direction but no one answered. Then I found two trucks that had keys in them. I got the second one started when a Union Pacific work train arrived. I abandoned the truck and flagged the train down. When I explained who I was and that I needed to get in touch with the U.S. Air Force at Hill Air Force Base in Utah, they contacted the base through their communications system and it was decided that they would take me to a place in Ogden where the U.S. Air Force could pick me up. Then we loaded up and headed toward Ogden—but not before we went and unloaded a couple of boxcars.

Epilogue

As I later thought about the Great Salt Lake, I remembered its surface is about 4,200 feet above sea level. Also, they tell me that our B-58's altimeter was lagging the actual altitude by several thousand feet. But the fact that I was ejecting at a much lower altitude than I thought did not occur to me at the time.

Walt and Ray did not make it, and we will never know why. I continued on in the flight-test business and flew the General Dynamics F-111 Aardvark and F-16 Falcon before I retired.

Ejection from a YB-58A Hustler: Part II,
by Monty Montgomery Jr.

The YB-58A (S/N 58-1020) was a prototype aircraft equipped with Convair ejection seats. It was later modified to become an operational Strategic Air Command aircraft and redesignated as B-58A. I was a U.S. Air Force captain, assigned to the 43rd Bomb Wing at Carswell Air Force Base in Texas. On December 27, 1961, my U.S. Air Force crew was Capt. Louis Hughes and bombardier/navigator Capt. John Roddy, as defensive system operator. Our mission that day was to conduct a high-altitude Mach 2 bombing run, followed by an aerial refueling and then a low-level bomb run.

We lifted off at about 4:30 P.M., completed the high-altitude bomb run, and picked up fuel from the tanker without any problems. We had about 41,000 pounds of fuel onboard and at about 9:00 P.M. we were preparing for the low-level bomb run. I was somewhat surprised to hear a female voice in my headset saying, "Left fuel manifest pressure low!" After scanning my instruments, I realized we were in big trouble! We were losing fuel rapidly with no way to stop the flow. Our nearest base was Whitman Air Force Base in Missouri, and Hughes gave me the steering direction. It was soon quite clear that at our rate of fuel loss we wouldn't make it. I gave the crew the bad news and advised them to get ready to eject.

We were about four miles northeast of Cole Camp, Missouri, at about 18,000 feet in altitude with an airspeed of about 285 knots, when one by one the engines flamed out from fuel starvation. Without power, the aircraft's systems began to shut down, and I signaled for ejection to begin. The ejection sequence began, starting with the DSO and working forward. By the time I squeezed the triggers within the ejection seat handles, the aircraft was in a 90 degree roll. The ejection seat did its job and my chute deployed automatically. But in my excitement, I forgot to deploy my survival kit after seat separation, and with this 50 pounds of additional weight I came in fast and hit the ground hard. It was a freezing night with a 30-mile-per-hour wind blowing, which gave me a lot of trouble in getting out of my parachute harness.

Off in the distance, I could see a light mounted on a pole and walked toward it. It turned out to be a farm with several cars parked in front of the house. From within the farmhouse I could hear talking and music and knocked on the door. In response to my knocking, the house suddenly became quite still and then I heard the sound of running, and finally a woman opened the door. She took one look at me and screamed. A man quickly came to the door and let me in. I didn't realize that I had cut my neck during the ejection, and with my helmet on and blood streaming down on my flight clothes I must have been quite a sight.

Fortunately there was a medical doctor among the group and he took me to his office in the nearby town of Cole. He treated me in his office and I called Whitman Air Force Base.

The same ejection sequence seen from the viewpoint of Louis Hughes.

After receiving the bailout order and the eject light came on, I waited for Rod (Capt. John Roddy) to go and as he went, I pulled the ejection trigger. The next sensation I had was that of floating with something bumping me on the back. I then realized that I had not separated from the ejection seat. I immediately tried to push myself away from the seat, which turned into quite a battle.

As I finally got clear, I pulled the ripcord and the chute opened. I looked down and the clear night air allowed me to see our burning aircraft on the ground. I later learned that I must have fallen 10,000 to 12,000 feet getting clear of the seat. This was determined by the fact that the cloud layer was at about 3,000 to 4,000 feet and I didn't get my parachute opened until I was below these clouds.

As I descended, there appeared to be numerous ponds and I was concerned about landing in water. As I approached the ground I dropped my survival kit down on its lanyard and brought my legs together, bending my knees slightly. I hit the ground relatively gently, but falling backwards, which caused me to bite my tongue. I was down in a low area very close to a pond with cows around me. What had appeared to be water from the air were bare spots where the snow had melted. At first I was cautious about moving, but within a few minutes a low-flying jet flew over me. About that time a bright light came on a distance up a hill from me.

It took me a few minutes to collect my senses. I detached my survival kit and, carrying it, I started walking toward the light. Walking was quite difficult because it was very dark, and I stumbled several times but kept making my way toward the light. I finally got close enough to see the light was on a pole outside a farmhouse. As I approached the house a big dog started barking furiously. I yelled several times with no results and it appeared that no one was home. I decided I needed to make friends with the dog so I could get to the front door. I thought of the can of Spam that I carried in my survival kit. I opened it, got the Spam out, and started feeding it to the dog. We were immediately friends.

With the now-friendly dog, I eased into the yard and up to the door. The lights were on and a phone was in plain sight on a table. I tried the door and it was unlocked. I called out several times, identifying myself and then walked over and picked up the phone. To my amazement, I heard Capt. Roddy talking. The phone was on a party line and he was at another house. After greeting him, Roddy put his host farmer on the line. I described the interior of the house, where about I was, and he knew exactly in which farmhouse I was. Within 20 minutes I was picked up and taken to Roddy. Later, after some celebration, we were driven to Whitman Air Force Base, where we were reunited with Captain Montgomery.

Author's Note

The accident investigation revealed that the electric starter on the number-two engine didn't disengage after engine start.

This locked the starter into the same speed as the turbojet engines, which exceeded its designed rotating speed. Eventually, the starter disintegrated and threw about high-velocity, shrapnel-like parts, some of which punctured the fuel manifold.

Montgomery's and Roddy's ejection seats worked as advertised, but this was not the case with Hughes' seat. It was discovered that the reason Hughes had problems getting clear of his ejection seat was a failure in the seat-separator strap. This separator strap (nicknamed a butt-snapper) failed to operate, as it had been burned in two by the ejection seat's rocket motor. A fix for this problem—the installation of a shield to protect the strap from the rocket flame—was installed on all the B-58s equipped with the Convair ejection seats.

This bailout event was the first time a full crew survived ejecting from a B-58. It was also amazing that in this night bailout the crew basically only had minor scrapes and bruises. Montgomery had a cut on his neck that required medical treatment and Hughes had a sore, bitten tongue and a finger cut from opening the can of Spam. Both Hughes and Roddy were relieved that the Air Force didn't require them to take a post-ejection blood test, because they had both celebrated their survival by imbibing at the friendly farmhouse Roddy had stumbled upon that night.

Ejecting in an Encapsulated Seat from a B-58A Hustler, by Clinton Ray Brisendine

On June 14, 1967, I was a U.S. Air Force major assigned to the 305th Bomber Wing of the Strategic Air Command at Bunker Hill Air Force Base in Indiana. That day's assignment was to conduct a practice low-level bomb run using radar bomb scoring. Our aircraft was a production-model Convair B-58A (S/N 61-2061), which was the 98th Hustler built in the series. Unlike the earlier ships, this one was fitted with Stanley Aviation encapsulated ejection seats. I was the pilot, with a U.S. Air Force crew consisting of Capt. William Bennett and navigator/bombardier Capt. Gary Cecchett, the defensive system operator (DSO).

We lifted off from Bunker Hill in the afternoon and were scheduled to rendezvous with a KC-135 tanker. We could see a thunderstorm ahead and Bennett was giving me steering commands to divert around the storm. We inadvertently flew through a squall line that contained large hailstones— big enough to shatter my windshield. While I was unhurt, the roar from the Mach 0.92 air forces was so severe that I couldn't communicate with my crew. I thought that the best approach would be to slow the aircraft by retarding the throttles, and then to manually encapsulate my seat. In this isolated environment I thought it should be quiet enough to allow communicating. My plan was to tell the crew of our situation and return to base, which would require steering information from Bennett. The first part of my plan worked perfectly. I reduced engine thrust and closed the doors to my capsule, controlling the aircraft flight using the flight control stick, which was located on the floor of my capsule. Now able to communicate with my crew, I told them of my situation and the plan to return to base. I attempted to open the capsule doors and discovered they were jammed shut.

In the B-58, each crew member was in his own compartment and there was no way they could help me in opening my capsule doors. Because I had reduced engine thrust prior to encapsulating, the aircraft was descending. The capsule contained an override switch for the throttle, but it could only be used to retard, not increase, the engine thrust levels. As I would raise the aircraft's nose in an attempt to slow the aircraft's rate of descent, the airspeed would fall off, approaching a stall. There was no way I could win this battle with the controlling laws of physics—I didn't have enough engine thrust to maintain flying speed.

My battle was lost, and I told my crew of the only option open being to eject. We were about six miles south southwest of Darrozett, Texas, when I told them it was time to go and they agreed. I held the ship in a stable descending mode and my crew ejected in the recommended order: rear to front with the DSO first, followed by the navigator/bombardier, and then myself. It turned out that I almost waited too late to eject. My capsule's parachute opened, the capsule took a couple of swings, and I hit the ground with a resounding thump—rolling almost inverted—and then stopped.

I was trapped within my capsule, but after a few minutes I heard a knock on the outside. This was followed by a welcome voice asking, "Is there anyone inside?" Then, "Are you all right?" It turned out that several people traveling in pickups down a road some distance away saw our ship crash.

The capsule doors were so jammed that it took several men to literally pound and pry the doors open. What a relief it was to be helped to step out and to stand up, with only some bruises. Then I was in for the second big shock for the day! My capsule had landed just a few feet from the edge of a cliff, which could have easily changed my safe landing into that of a disaster.

Epilogue

Other than some scrapes and bruises, I was fine, as was my DSO, Capt. Gary Cecchett. He landed within walking distance of my landing spot and we were quickly reunited. Unfortunately, this was not the case for my navigator/bombardier, Capt. William Bennett. His capsule's parachute failed to open and he was killed as his plummeting capsule slammed into the ground.

U.S. Air Force/NAA B-70 Valkyrie
Intercontinental Bomber

NAA XB-70A was a four-place, Mach 3, 80,000-foot-altitude, six-engine, delta-wing intercontinental bomber. Ship number one (S/N 62-001) was first flown on September 21, 1964, from Palmdale Airport in Palmdale, California. NAA Chief Test Pilot Alvin S. White, along with U.S. Air Force Col. Joseph Cotton as copilot, were at the controls. Only two ships were completed and in this experimental configuration it was a two-place aircraft. Each crew member sat in an encapsulated seat, designed and built by NAA.

This North American Aviation XB-70A Valkyrie triplesonic bomber, the first of two built, is presently on display at the U.S. Air Force Museum in Dayton, Ohio. The second ship was lost in a midair collision. In this photo, the wing tips are in their full-down position. *North American Aviation*

In addition to the encapsulated seat being a means of escape from this high-performance aircraft, it would provide the crew with other important features. The crew would now fly in what was termed a shirtsleeve environment, meaning the crew would no longer be required to wear full-pressure suits. Wearing standard flight clothes, they would be able to leave their seats to stretch, eat, or make use of the toilet, located aft of the bombardier/navigator station (planned for the

North American Aviation Chief Test Pilot Alvin S. White stands next to an operational mock-up of the encapsulated ejection seat used on the XB-70A Valkyrie bomber. White was the first flight pilot in command of the two ships built. White used the encapsulated seat to eject from the disabled aircraft. *North American Aviation*

production A/C). In the event of the loss of cockpit pressurization, each crew member could close his capsule doors to form an airtight enclosure, pressurized with oxygen to the equivalent of 8,000 feet in altitude. From within the capsule, a window allowed the pilot and copilot visual access to their instrument panels. Within each of these capsules was a handheld

The pillowlike inflated devices on the side and top of the XB-70A Valkyrie encapsulated seat are manually deployed flotation bags for use in the event of a water landing. The cylindrical device on the bottom is the impact attenuator, which is designed to soak up landing loads. *North American Aviation*

Shown here is an XB-70A encapsulated seat undergoing a flotation test. Note that the impact attenuator has served its function and is deflated. *North American Aviation*

"pickle" control. By the use of the pickle, either pilot could control the flight of the aircraft and retard the throttles. Thus, in the event of a loss of cabin pressurization, they could fly the aircraft down to an altitude to where the crew could open their capsule doors and resume flight in a normal manner.

Another advantage to the encapsulated seat was that in the event of ejection, each crew member would be provided with his own survival shelter. The shelter would protect from heat, cold, and wind, and also serve as a life raft. The capsule was self-righting from any attitude, even without inflating the supplementary flotation bladders. Stored within the capsule was

50 pounds of food, water, a survival radio, and survival gear, including arctic clothing, a .22-caliber hunting rifle, matches, fishing gear, a signaling mirror, and flares.

Each encapsulated crew seat operated independently from a handle on each side of the seat. Pulling up either handle disconnected and stowed the control wheel and retracted the seat and shoulder harness, which pulled the crew member back into the capsule, where the upper and lower doors closed and the capsule pressurized. Pulling up the handle exposed the ejection trigger. Squeezing either trigger jettisoned the hatch and ignited the rocket motor. As the seat moved up the ejection rails, an air-data input tripper armed the seat as to either high or low speed. In 0.4 seconds the seat cleared the upper end of the ejection rails and 0.5 seconds later, the two telescoping stabilizers were extended; in 1.5 seconds the drogue chutes, stowed within the stabilizers, were deployed.

At 15,000 feet the parachute deployed. If the seat was in a low-speed mode, the chute was deployed "unreefed." If the tripper had set the seat to the high-speed mode, the chute deployed in a "reefed" condition for two seconds and then the reef line was cut, allowing full opening. The "reefed" position was to reduce the parachute opening loads at high speed. At the same time the chute was deployed, the impact attenuator bag was deployed and the emergency locator beacon activated. On the ground, a manual system allowed crew members to sever the parachute risers and deploy the flotation bags.

The encapsulated seat had a capability range of zero altitude/zero velocity up to the maximum flight envelope of the XB-70A. The ejected weight of the seat was 470 pounds. The ring-sail parachute built by Pioneer Parachute was 34.5 feet in diameter.

One may wonder why, with all its positive features, we no longer see encapsulated ejection seats in present aircraft design. There are several reasons. The major reasons are that

The first of six photos illustrating an encapsulated ejection seat test for the XB-70A Valkyrie, here the rocket catapult thrust tails off with the stabalization booms extended. The following five pages show the remainder of the sequence. *North American Aviation*

2

Drag chutes deploy from stabalization booms as drogue chute deploys main recovery parachute. *North Amercian Aviation*

Drogue chute has extended main recovery chute suspension lines. *North Amercian Aviation*

Main recovery chute opens in reefed condition and impact attenuator has inflated. *North Amercian Aviation*

5

Main recovery chute has fully inflated and escape capsule is ready for landing. *North Amercian Aviation*

Encapsulated seat is landing with impact attenuator decelerating the capsule impact by controlled deflation. *North Amercian Aviation*

Shown here is an XB-70A Valkyrie encapsulated seat moments prior to touchdown during a test at Edwards Air Force Base in California. *North American Aviation*

the encapsulated seat weighs at least three times as much as an advanced ejection seat and comes with a commensurate increase in cost. Due to encapsulated seats being more complex, maintenance costs are much higher than an advanced ejection seat. Another negative aspect to the encapsulated seat is its intrusion into the available crew station space. As an example, on the XB-70A the cockpit center pedestal had to be spring-counterbalanced and hinged up much like that of a drawbridge to allow ingress and egress in or out of the crew seats. Even with the hinged center pedestal, a thermally cooled assist handle was required in the cockpit overhead to allow the crew to swing around and into their seats. Naturally, these provisions also added to the weight and cost.

Ejecting from the XB-70A Valkyrie

On June 8, 1966, at 7:15 A.M., North American Chief Test Pilot Alvin S. White released the brakes on XB-70A, ship number two, for takeoff from Edwards Air Force Base in California. U.S. Air Force Maj. Carl S. Cross had finished his ground school and preliminary flight training and was making his first flight in the XB-70A, as copilot.

After the scheduled testing was completed, the XB-70A joined a flight of five airplanes at 8:45 A.M. at an altitude of 20,000 feet. The purpose of the flight was to take formation photos of General Electric-powered aircraft. The ships in formation were (left to right) the Northrop T-38 Talon; McDonnell F-4 Phantom II; XB-70A; Lockheed F-104 Starfighter, flown by NASA pilot Joseph A. Walker; and the Northrop F-5 Freedom Fighter. Another aircraft was a contracted Learjet photographic airplane flying loosely in formation with and to the extreme left of the other five ships. The ships climbed to 25,000 feet and were in a loose "V," with the XB-70A in front at the center.

At 9:26 A.M., the NASA F-104 collided with the XB-70A from a position below and overlapping the XB-70A. The initial contact was between the left horizontal stabilizer of the F-104 and the canted right wing tip of the XB-70A. After this contact, the F-104 pitched up and rolled to the left, struck the leading edge of the XB-70A's right wing, and continued to roll, inverted, across the top of the XB-70A, damaging the right vertical stabilizer and shearing off its left vertical. The impact cut or broke the F-104 just behind the cockpit. Its nose section hit the XB-70A's left wing, and the F-104's fuselage section streamed off the XB-70A in flames.

EJECT!

Even though the XB-70A had been mortally wounded, the inertia of the giant bird, together with its flight control augmentation system, carried it on in stable flight as though nothing had happened. Neither White nor Cross was aware that their ship had been struck. They thought the loud thump, explosion, and yell of "midair," and, "Joe Walker ran into him!" applied to other aircraft in the formation. Meanwhile, the severed hydraulic lines that fed the Valkyrie's vertical stabilizer actuators (vital to the craft's flight-control systems) were pumping their lifeblood fluids overboard. Thus, after being struck five times by the F-104, the XB-70A flew on for another 16 seconds.

But with the last of the hydraulic fluid gone, the flight controls no longer responded to White's inputs. The great ship yawed violently to the right and did a snap roll. The force was so violent that White thought the ship's nose would break off. The ship came upright and then snap-rolled again, this time tearing off a major portion of the damaged left wing, and entered a flat spin.

All of this did not go well for White; for Cross it did not go at all. The violent "eyeballs-out" acceleration forces made it extremely difficult for White to reach the ejection handles. He was able to finally grasp and pull the right handle. This forcibly tightened his shoulder harness, pulled the seat back into the capsule and slammed the capsule doors shut. Immediately, White felt excruciating pain. Due to the side loads in the flat-spin, his right elbow was trapped outside the door closure envelope. If he ejected now, there was a chance his right elbow could be torn off, as the capsule rocketed through the hatch opening. Using his left hand, he was able to pry his right-hand fingers out of the ejection handle, pull his elbow inside, and squeeze the ejection trigger. The ejection hatch successfully fired, and the capsule blasted away from the doomed XB-70A. While attempting to get his fingers free,

White could see Cross struggling to eject, but it was impossible for him to help.

White remembers the blast of cold air through the open capsule doors as he ejected. Since he was now below 15,000 feet, the capsule parachute opened immediately. As he looked out, the spinning XB-70A nose swung by, seemingly only inches away. White closed the capsule doors for two reasons: first, so as not to see the spinning plane, and second, to manually deploy the impact attenuation air bag to cushion his ground impact. The impact attenuator is located between the lower door and capsule. When the capsule doors are open, automatic inflation is inhibited during the ejection sequence. Without the impact attenuator, there was a strong possibility that ground impact while still in the capsule would result in a broken back.

White was still disoriented and concerned about a lot of things: whether Carl Cross was able to eject, the junk falling around him, and a terrible coldness (probably from shock). He couldn't remember which control manually inflated the impact attenuation air bag and he also knew one of the capsule controls would release the parachute riser. Not wanting to do anything wrong, he accepted the fate of a hard landing. About this time the XB-70A hit about a mile away from him and exploded, with an enormous plume of smoke rising into the air.

"I saw a big Joshua tree coming up and thought, 'God, I'm going in fast.'" Then, without its inflated impact attenuator bag, the escape capsule, with White inside, slammed down on a rocky slope. Nearby was the XB-70A's severed left wing, located about a mile from the main wreckage. Fortunately, the capsule struck on its edge, and—combined with the seat fasten failing—this cushioned White's landing and prevented further injury.

Inside the capsule, which had flopped over on its side and faced downhill, White forced his tormented body to fight free. One of the survival packs in the capsule had broken loose and had his helmeted head clamped down. Pinned down on his injured right arm, he had only his left hand with which to work. He got the capsule door open once, only to have it snap closed again. On his next try White took off his helmet and, after opening the door again, wedged his helmet into the opening. He was able to climb out and wave at two T-38s making low passes overhead.

After climbing out of the capsule, shock really set in, and White was sweating and bone cold. He retrieved his flight jacket from the capsule, but he was still cold. He staggered up the slope and wrapped himself in the capsule parachute.

About 35 minutes later, the first helicopter arrived to aid White. Instead of landing, the rugged terrain forced the helicopter to hover over White to pick him up. The downwash from the rotor blades inflated the capsule parachute and White almost became airborne again. Seeing the problem, the chopper moved about 50 yards away and dropped a rescue team. They put White on a stretcher and flew him back to Edwards Air Force Base Hospital.

Author's Note

A postcrash photo analysis revealed that Bob Walker's F-104 was below and overlapping the XB-70A's right wing. Walker allowed his F-104 to move into a position relative to the XB-70A, from which recovery was impossible. He was killed instantly as his inverted aircraft struck the vertical stabilizer of the XB-70. White made a complete recovery and returned to flight status. In relation to Carl Cross, it could not be determined whether he was unable to reach his seat's ejection handle or whether the "eyeballs-out" (-Gx) g-forces exceeded the escape system's capability to pull him and his seat back into the capsule to eject. Cross was killed when the XB-70A, with his capsule still inside, crashed into the desert floor. XB-70A, aircraft number one, the only surviving aircraft, is on display at the Air Force Museum in Dayton, Ohio.

Chapter Fourteen

CREW ESCAPE MODULES

C rew escape modules were used in multiplace aircraft to solve the problem of possible collisions between canopies/hatches and the ejecting crew members and their ejection seats. Crew modules also provided ground or sea shelters for post-ejected crew awaiting rescue.

U.S. Air Force/Convair F-111A Aardvark Fighter-Bomber

The F-111A was a two-place, twin-engine, swing-wing fighter-bomber, which was first flown on December 21, 1964, from Fort Worth, Texas. The pilot was Richard Johnson, who was assisted by flight-test engineer Van E. Prahl. The first 11 F-111s were equipped with a pair of Douglas Escapac I-1 ejection seats, while the development and qualification of the crew escape module (being built by McDonnell Aircraft) was ongoing. Several versions of this aircraft were built, including a model designed to operate from aircraft carriers and as a fighter-bomber, with a total of 542 of all models built. Ship number 12 and subsequent aircraft were provided with McDonnell crew escape modules.

The General Dynamics F-111F Aardvark fighter-bomber was equipped with a crew escape module built by McDonnell Aircraft. *General Dynamics, via Lockheed Martin*

With the crew escape module, either crewman could initiate the completely automatic ejection process. Upon initiation, the inertia reel harness for each man was tightened to position and restrained each during ejection, and the emergency oxygen was simultaneously activated. The next step in the sequence was to separate the crew escape module from the remainder of the fuselage. A splice plate with a linear-shaped charge covered the periphery between the crew module and the fuselage structure. The shape charge, together with explosive bolts, severed the two components. A rocket motor pushed the module away from the aircraft as lanyards pulled apart the remaining electrical and mechanical connections to the aircraft.

Shown here is a General Dynamics F-111 Aardvark's crew escape module after an inflation test of its self-righting and flotation bags. *General Dynamics*

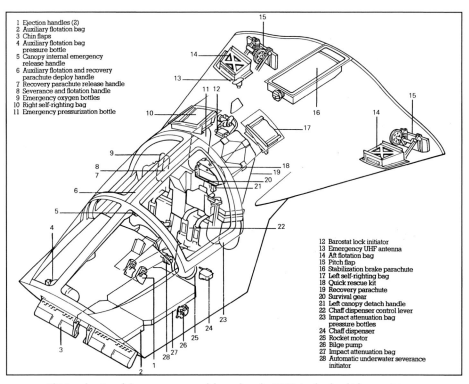

1 Ejection handles (2)
2 Auxiliary flotation bag
3 Chin flaps
4 Auxiliary flotation bag
   pressure bottle
5 Canopy internal emergency
   release handle
6 Auxiliary flotation and recovery
   parachute deploy handle
7 Recovery parachute release handle
8 Severance and flotation handle
9 Emergency oxygen bottles
10 Right self-righting bag
11 Emergency pressurization bottle

12 Barostat lock initiator
13 Emergency UHF antenna
14 Aft flotation bag
15 Pitch flap
16 Stabilization brake parachute
17 Left self-righting bag
18 Quick rescue kit
19 Recovery parachute
20 Survival gear
21 Left canopy detach handle
22 Chaff dispenser control lever
23 Impact attenuation bag
   pressure bottles
24 Chaff dispenser
25 Rocket motor
26 Bilge pump
27 Impact attenuation bag
28 Automatic underwater severance
   initiator

This is a drawing of the crew escape module used on the F-111 Aardvark, which was a joint effort between McDonnell Aircraft and General Dynamics. *General Dynamics, via Lockheed Martin*

A mortar deployed a drogue chute to stabilize the module, placing it in a nose-down descent. As the module passed through 14,000 feet in altitude, the Steinthall ring-sail recovery parachute was deployed. Via a tear-out strip, the deployment of the recovery parachute repositioned the module into a normal horizontal position, and the impact attenuation air bags were deployed. The last step in this automated sequence was inflation of the flotation bags upon landing impact. A manual handle was provided to allow the crew to sever the recovery parachute bridles subsequent to landing.

This photo of a test of the Aardvark F-111's crew escape module shows how small the module seems in relation to its Steinthall ring-sail recovery parachute. *General Dynamics*

EJECT!

Ejecting from an F-111 Aardvark

It was October 19, 1967, and David J. Thigpen was an engineering test pilot for General Dynamics. He and flight-test engineer Max Gordon were assigned to perform a loads test on the speed brake of an F-111A, ship number 15, Air Force S/N 63-9780. On the F-111, the forward section of the main landing gear doors also functioned as a speed brake. During this test, the use of increased airspeeds would incrementally increase the loads on the speed brake—a test not considered to be hazardous. In addition to the structural test on the speed brakes, this flight was also to observe the impact that speed-brake operation had on engine performance. The flight was to be monitored not only by the onboard flight engineer, but also on the ground via telemetry and radio voice contact. These functions were conducted from the Fort Worth Center by a team of engineers headed by Dale Ford.

While the earlier F-111s were equipped with ejection seats, this ship had a crew escape module built by McDonnell Aircraft. On this particular test aircraft, a large flight-test camera console was located between the side-by-side seated crew, which prevented crew members from seeing one another. This aircraft had special mirrors installed to monitor deployment of the side brake.

The crew lifted off from Carswell Air Force Base/Fort Worth Airport in Texas and completed a number of flight-control tests. Upon completion, they climbed to altitude to begin the speed-brake tests. As the flight loads on the speed-brake deployment were incrementally increased, coordination took place between the flight crew and the ground telemetry monitoring team. To this point, the testing had gone by the book. At a speed of Mach 1.77 and at 39,000 feet in altitude, Thigpen deployed the speed brakes once again, but this time the results were quite different. The doors opened to about 60 degrees and then slammed shut with a muffled bang.

CREW ESCAPE MODULES

Several other anomalies occurred and Thigpen saw that the hydraulic pressure in the primary system was rapidly dropping from 3,000 psi toward zero. At the time, they were about 50 to 60 miles northwest of Carswell, and Thigpen began a gentle left descending turn to head back to base. He requested and received a clearance back to the Fort Worth Center.

During this turn he noticed the pressure in the utility system begin to fall also. In about 20 seconds the utility pressure had dropped to 1,200 psi, and Thigpen began to lose control of the aircraft. As the F-111 has only two systems to operate its flight controls, the loss of the second is life threatening. As the second system failed, the aircraft began to twitch and then its actions became more violent. Thigpen attempted to control this with his stick, but it was useless. Ground test control recommended they abandon the aircraft.

The aircraft flew for about 30 seconds, all the while losing speed and eventually becoming subsonic, and for a few seconds was generally in a wings-level mode.

Thigpen said, "Now!" The ejection sequence seemed to take minutes to begin, but in reality was only about 1/3 of a second. There was a loud bang as the linear-shaped charge severed the module from the fuselage and its escape rocket fired. The forces of ejection were felt, but they weren't excessive. Ejection was followed shortly by the deployment of the drogue chute. Prior to this, while in the U.S. Navy, Thigpen had bailed out of an LTV F-8 Crusader in its Martin-Baker ejection seat. He thought the separation of the F-111 was much milder than ejecting with the Martin-Baker seat.

The module was now pointing almost straight down toward the ground and rotated slowly; the only two instruments still functioning were the clock and altimeter. Thigpen and Gordon timed their rotation speed and determined that they were rotating every 10 seconds.

As they passed through 14,000 feet, the main parachute was deployed and they saw the repositioning bridle being snapped out from its center-beam stowage. The module then repositioned into a normal flight condition. With their main chute deployed, their descent was slowed and they lost sight of their aircraft. A gunpowder smell from the detonating cord permeated the cabin. Their mood became even more surrealistic as they opened their side windows to ventilate the cabin and took off their helmets; Gordon even unbuckled himself so

Shown here is a crew escape module built by McDonnell Aircraft for the F-111 Aardvark. This is the type of crew module that David Thigpen used to escape from his ailing F-111.
McDonnell Aircraft, via Boeing Historical Archives

he could reach the F-111's checklist, which had fallen forward during their vertical descent. Both crew members commented as to how slowly they appeared to be descending, so ultimately the clock and altimeter were used to calculate their rate of descent.

Thigpen had misjudged their height, and while readjusting himself back into his seat they smacked onto the ground. The capsule slowly rotated over onto its side. While the impact with the ground was solid, it was obvious that the attenuation air bags on the bottom of the module did their job.

The crew then saw something that made them wonder if they had survived all this only to die another way—their parachute had drooped across some nearby high-voltage wires. Gordon quickly pulled the parachute-severance handle, and the possible high-voltage electrical path was gone. They later found out that the "high-voltage" wires were merely telephone lines.

Both crew members were uninjured.

Author's Note

Postcrash investigation revealed that the landing gear door/speed brake had structurally failed. When the landing-gear door/speed brake failed it slammed closed, severing hydraulic lines in both systems. These lines were subsequently rerouted out of the landing gear bay to provide better protection, and the landing gear door/speed-brake structure was "beefed up."

U.S. Air Force/Rockwell International B-1A Bomber

The Rockwell B-1 was a four-place, blended swing-wing Mach 2 bomber. Rockwell Chief Test Pilot Charlie Bock—assisted by U.S. Air Force Col. Ted Sturmthal as copilot and Dick Abrams as flight-test engineer—was at the controls for its maiden flight. This flight (Air Force S/N 74-0158) took place

The first three Rockwell International B-1A bombers were equipped with a crew escape module. Starting with the fourth, the design was changed to utilize upward ejection seats. *Rockwell International*

from Palmdale Airport in Palmdale, California, on December 23, 1974.

The B-1 was an intercontinental bomber equipped for aerial refueling. In addition to its long-range capabilities, the aircraft was designed for long loiter periods, in the event of the threat of war. The aircraft's basic mission was termed as a "high-low-high," meaning high altitude to the area of the strike, a low-level penetration to the target, and then a high-altitude flight home. The mission scenario dictated long airborne flight hours. Due to long flight hours, the crew area had a number of specific features, including a galley, bunks, toilet, and a self-contained oxygen-generating system. To complement these features was what was termed a shirtsleeve environment. Instead of pressure suits, the crew wore standard flight clothes, which provided them with maximum comfort and physical freedom for ideal performance on extended missions. The first three B-1s were equipped with a crew escape module, allowing for recovery of the entire crew by ejection.

CREW ESCAPE MODULES

The ejectable crew module formed an integral portion of the aircraft forward fuselage. These subsystems were necessary to separate the module and provide a means of emergency escape and safe recovery of the crew. The ejectable module weighed almost 10,000 pounds and provided a post-ejection shelter for the crew as well as provisions for life support until rescue could be effected.

Ejection could be independently initiated by the pilot, copilot, or the two aft crew members working in unison. Each crew member had an ejection handle on his respective side consoles. Under normal conditions, the pilot would alert the

This is the crew escape module for the Rockwell International B-1A bomber. The two rocket motors not only separated and lifted the module away from the aircraft, they also performed the duty of controlling pitch and roll of the module. *Rockwell International*

The B-1A crew escape module successfully completes a water qualification test. It was at this same facility that the drop tests for the Apollo command module were made.
Rockwell International

crew of an impending ejection by depressing a push-button on his instrument panel, which illuminated a warning light on each of the crew member's instrument panels, sending a bailout signal to each crew member's headset, and by activating an alarm bell in the cabin. Upon squeezing the ejection handle(s), as described above, the completely automatic ejection sequence began.

During the first step of the sequence, the shoulder harness inertia reel on each seat was retracted to position to restrain each crew member in his seat. Simultaneously, the emergency oxygen and maneuvering rocket-control systems were activated. A linear-shaped charge, together with guillotines, lanyards, and explosive bolts, severed the crew module from the remaining fuselage structure and the pitch-and-roll rocket motors were ignited. As soon as adequate structural clearance was achieved, the nose spoiler and two stabilizing fins were erected and a mortar fired a 9-foot-diameter conical ribbon drogue chute. Upon safe "q" limits, the two side spoilers were deployed and the drogue chute released. Then twin mortars deployed the two pilot chutes, which extracted the three 50-foot ring-sail main chutes, which opened in a reefed condition. At this point the module was in a nose-down condition.

Reefing cutters then allowed full inflation of the main parachutes, and explosive bolts fired to reposition the module into a stable, level attitude. The jettisoning of the two rocket motors and the inflation of the five landing attenuation bladders followed. At this point, the crew escape module was ready for ground impact at approximately 29 feet per second. Manual controls allowed for main parachute jettison after landing. In the event of a water landing, manual controls provided for inflation of flotation and uprighting bladders.

As part of its qualification testing, the B-1A module was dropped from a Boeing B-52. The stabilization devices have been deployed and the deflated impact attenuators are projecting from the corners of the module. The empty cavities on the rear of the module are where the drogue and recovery parachutes were stored. *Rockwell International*

The B-1 module was a zero altitude/zero velocity system, allowing safe ejection from a parked position on the ground and throughout the aircraft's flight envelope.

With all of the positive features of an ejectable crew module, one would expect that this feature would be incorporated in the latest aircraft coming off the production lines. But this is not the case. There are a number of reasons why ejection seats, not crew modules, are on the latest U.S. aircraft. One reason is that the periodic change-out of the age-sensitive pyrotechnic devices used in this system grew to the point to be maintenance-cost prohibitive. The use of a crew module also had a major impact on the aircraft weight and severely limited future equipment additions to extend the aircraft's service life. Thus, after the first three B-1s were built, it was decided to redesign the aircraft and utilize four McDonnell Douglas ACES II ejection seats. Subsequently, Rockwell International received a contract for 100 additional subsonic versions of the B-1, which utilized ACES II ejection seats built by Weber Aircraft and were designated as B-1Bs. The B-1B was stealthier and designed to carry more external stores. At this point, the first four B-1s were then redesignated as B-1As.

Ejecting with the B-1A Crew Module, by Merv Evenson

On August 29, 1984, B-1A aircraft number two was scheduled for a test flight to evaluate dynamic air minimum control speed. These tests involve abruptly reducing/cutting thrust on one or two engines on one side of the aircraft and evaluating aircraft controllability. U.S. Air Force Maj. Dick Reynolds was the pilot, assisted by Rockwell Chief Test Pilot Doug Benefield as copilot. The flight-test engineer for this flight was U.S. Air Force Capt. Otto J. Waniczzek. The first chase aircraft was a General Dynamic F-111D, being flown by Rockwell Engineering Test Pilot Merv Evenson, accompanied by U.S. Air Force Capt. Steve Fraley as navigator/photographer. Prior to flight, the B-1 was taken out onto the taxiways to conduct some stress tests on its landing gear while performing short-radius taxi turns. Subsequent to this ground test, it was determined that one of the tires should be replaced, delaying takeoff.

Once flight took off from Edwards Air Force Base in California at 9:29 A.M., the performance testing began. One of these tests required checking handling qualities with the aircraft in an aft center-of-gravity condition. On the B-1, as with most aircraft, the center of gravity was kept within normal limits via proper fuel management. In this case, the most forward and aft fuel tanks were used to balance the aircraft by the use of an automatic fuel management system. To implement this test phase, the fuel management system was used to pump fuel farther aft than normal. At the conclusion of this test, the aircraft was being reconfigured for the next test phase, which was dynamic air minimum control speed evaluations.

During this test phase, the aircraft exhibited a slight nose rise characteristic of reaching the angle-of-attack limit, until it abruptly pitched nose-up to approximately 70 degrees. This violent departure from controlled flight put the wing well above any flyable angle of attack. At the apex of the pitch-up, the aircraft yawed left and right a cycle or two, then sliced off to the right, nose below the horizon and about 160 degrees off its original heading. The ship actually entered into a spin and it was obvious the only option was to eject. At about 10:23 A.M. Reynolds initiated ejection, at approximately 1,505 feet above ground level.

Instead of the crew module landing in a normal horizontal mode on its impact attenuation air bags, it landed on its forward right corner. This subjected the module and its occupants to excessive loads, actually causing the almost 10,000-pound module to spring or bounce back a number of feet. Reynolds and Waniczzek were severely injured and Benefield's condition was critical. Reynolds could see that Benefield was in great distress. Even though unable to rise and in a great deal of pain, Reynolds reached across to unlatch Benefield's seat harness to ease his stress. He then jettisoned his left window to signal to the chase plane circling overhead.

CREW ESCAPE MODULES

The same ejection sequence seen from the viewpoint of the chase plane.

On that fateful day of August 1984, I was assigned as first chase for the testing of B-1 bomber ship number two. After takeoff, the B-1 was configured for some routine trim checks and began to configure for the first test point. Since we had reached the eastern boundary of our test area, a left turn was taken to head back west. It was during this turn that the B-1 was being configured for the test points. Things seem to be going smoothly. My attention was averted from the B-1 as Edwards Air Force Base radar trackers notified us that six McDonnell F-4 aircraft were approaching our position from the north. When I was satisfied that we would remain clear of the aircraft, I looked back to the B-1. I immediately noticed it was in a nose-high attitude and called the aircrew to see if they were having a problem.

The answer came back, "We might have to punch!" It became apparent that they had slowed, and I couldn't fly that slow in my craft. I made a short zigzag to keep them in sight. When I turned back into the B-1's last position, it had already impacted the ground. I cannot remember if I heard the crew say they were going to eject.

I immediately notified the authorities and got air-rescue alerted. I then began to circle the B-1 and saw that the crew escape capsule was on the ground several hundred feet from the wreckage. I could spot it by the main chutes that were draped by the crew module. I assisted in directing some of the ground vehicles to the desert site, and after the helicopters had everything in order we went back to Edwards Air Force Base and landed.

Author's Note

A postcrash investigation revealed that, due to a problem with the fuel-management system, the aircraft experienced an aft center-of-gravity condition, which exceeded the restoring capability of the flight-control system. The incorrect positioning of the crew module for landing was due to the failure of one of the parachute-repositioning explosive bolts on the crew module to function. The crew module impacted the desert floor in a right, nose-down attitude instead of in a normal level-flight attitude. In this position, the module's impact attenuation air bags could not perform their required function of absorbing the ground impact. While both Air Force crew members sustained serious injuries, they recovered. Reynolds was able to return to flight status and is now a lieutenant general in the U.S. Air Force and commander of the Aeronautical Systems Center at Wright-Patterson Air Force Base in Ohio. Waniczzek is in the U.S. Air Force Reserves as a test pilot school instructor and is employed full time with an aircraft manufacturer. Unfortunately, Doug Benefield did not survive.

In 2000, the recovered crew module from aircraft number two was in the process of being restored for display at the Edwards Air Force Base Museum. Aircraft number one has been disassembled and is used as a test vehicle at the Newport Antenna Research Facility at the Air Force Research Lab's Rome Research Site in New York. The last of the crew module–equipped B-1s is aircraft number three, which is on display at The Wings Over The Rockies Air and Space Museum in Denver, Colorado.

Chapter Fifteen

EJECTION SEATS BY MANUFACTURER

A uthor's note: A review of the following list will sometimes show that more than one manufacturer provided
ejection seats for a given aircraft.

Aircraft Mechanics, Inc. Aircraft Mechanics built the upward
ejecting seats for the Convair F-106 Delta Dart; Douglas
Aircraft B-66 Destroyer; Glenn L. Martin B-57A Intruder;
NAA F-100D Super Sabre; and the Republic F-84F
Thunderjet and F-105 Thunderchief.

Aircraft Mechanics, Inc., later became part of B.F. Goodrich's
UPCO (Universal Propulsion Co.). At the time this book
was written, B.F. Goodrich owned the rights to all the ejection seats built in the United States. The only exception

would be if the Martin-Baker Co. receives a contract to provide ejection seats for the U.S. military F-22 or the Joint Strike Fighter. If that occurs, the Martin-Baker Co. has agreed they will assemble their seats in the United States, not only for these programs, but for the Raytheon T-6 Texan II turboprop-powered trainer.

Bell Aircraft Bell Aircraft built the ejection seat for their X-1B research aircraft and the jettisonable nose on their X-2 research aircraft.

Convair (General Dynamics) Convair, later a division of General Dynamics, designed and built the ejection seats for their XP-81, XB-46, XF-92A, XF2Y-1 Sea Dart, XFY-1 Pogo, and B-58 Hustler.

Douglas Aircraft Co. Douglas Aircraft was the leading ejection seat manufacturer in the United States. Their seats were manufactured under the names of RAPEC, Escapac, STAPAC, and ACES. Except for Martin-Baker, Douglas probably built more ejection seats than any other company in the world. Some of the aircraft that utilized Douglas escape systems were the following: the Bell XV-15 and Bell XV-22A Osprey; the Douglas D-558-2 Skyrocket, F3D Skyknight, A2D-1 Skyshark, F4D Skyray, X-3 Stiletto, A3D Skywarrior, A4D Skyhawk, F5D Skylancer, LTV XC-142A V/STOL, and LTV A-7 Corsair II; the McDonnell Douglas F-15 Eagle, F/A-18 Hornet, and T-45 Goshawk; the Glenn L. Martin B-57F Intruder; the Fairchild A-10 Thunderbolt II (nicknamed Warthog); the Boeing/Lockheed Martin F-22 Raptor; the Rockwell International B-1 (ship number four); the General Dynamics Model 48 Charger, F-16 Fighting Falcon, and F-111 Aardvark; the Ryan Aircraft XV-5B Vertifan; the Northrop B-2 Spirit; and the Lockheed F-117 Stealth Fighter and XV-4B Hummingbird. Later, Douglas Aircraft merged and became McDonnell Douglas and then, later yet, Boeing.

Later still, the McDonnell Douglas ACES II ejection seat system was sold to B.F. Goodrich's Universal Propulsion Co. Division (UPCO).

Grumman Aircraft Grumman designed and built the ejection seat for the XF9F-6 Cougar. Later, Grumman turned to Martin-Baker for all their ejection seat–equipped aircraft.

Lockheed Aircraft Lockheed Aircraft built the ejection seats for their P-80C Shooting Star, the T-33 Silverstar, XF-90, F-94 Starfire, XV-1 Salmon, F-104 Starfighter, U-2, A-12, XV-4A Hummingbird, SR-71 Blackbird, S-3A Viking, and the Boeing/Lockheed Martin F-22 Raptor. Some of these seats were built under license from Stanley Aviation.

Ling Temco Vought LTV built the seats for their XF8U-1 Crusader.

Glenn L. Martin Aircraft Martin built the ejection seats for their XB-51, B-57 Canberra, and the XP6M-1 Seamaster.

Martin-Baker Some of the American aircraft fitted with Martin-Baker ejection seats were the Bell V-22 Osprey; the Grumman A2F-1/A-6 Intruder, T-45 Goshawk, F-14 Tomcat, and F9F Cougar; the Lockheed T-33 Silverstar and LTV XF8U-1/F-8 Crusader; the McDonnell F4H-1/F-4 Phantom, F3H Demon, and the F/A-18 Hornet; and the NAA FJ-4 Fury.

At the time of the writing, Martin-Baker has offered to assemble their ejection seats within the United States so they can remain an acceptable source for future American military aircraft ejection seats. In 2000, Martin-Baker was a strong contender in providing their Mark 16E ejection seat for the Lockheed Martin proposal for the Joint Strike Fighter.

McDonnell Aircraft Corp. McDonnell relied on others to build their escape systems. The exception was the crew escape module McDonnell Aircraft built for the Convair F-111 Aardvark.

North American Aviation, Inc. This company was quite unique, in that beginning with their XB-45 Tornado bomber in 1947, the company designed and installed the escape systems for almost all their aircraft, up until the B-1A, ship number four, in 1979. The only NAA aircraft not equipped with an NAA ejection seat was the FJ-4 Fury, which used a Martin-Baker seat. In addition to building ejection seats for their own aircraft, they supplied some of the seats for the McDonnell F-101 Voodoo.

NAA provided the escape systems for their F-86 Sabres, XAJ-1 Savages, YF-93A, XA2J-1, FJ-2 Fury, F-100 Super Sabre, FJ-3 Fury, YF-107A, T2J-1 Buckeye, A3J/A5/RA-5 Vigilante, X-15 research aircraft, XB-70A Valkyrie, OV-10 Bronco, and the B-1A (ships number one, two, and three). Later, NAA became part of Rockwell International and then, later yet, Boeing

Northrop Aircraft Co. The first Northrop Aircraft equipped with an ejection seat was their XP/F-89 Scorpion fighter-interceptor, which utilized a Northrop-designed and -built ejection seat. This followed their YT-38 Talon trainer and YF-5 Freedom Fighter. Later, Northrop used other manu-facturers' ejection seats in their aircraft.

Republic Aviation Republic built the ejection seats for their RF-84F Thunderflash XF-91 and some of the seats for their F-105 Thunderchief. In addition, Republic built some of the ejection seats for the Boeing B-47 Stratofortress.

Stanley Aviation Corp. In 1949, Stanley Aviation received a contract to design and build the standard U.S. Air Force downward ejection seat, plus other ejection seats for the U.S. Air Force. The contract resulted in that company building over 2,800 seats. Some of the aircraft equipped with the Stanley seat were the Boeing B-52 Stratofortress (downward ejecting); the Convair F-102 Delta Dagger and F-106 Delta Dart; the Douglas RB-66 Destroyer (downward ejecting); the Lockheed F-104 Starfighter; and the Martin P6M-1 Seamaster.

In addition, Stanley developed the YANKEE system, which was retrofitted into many Douglas A-1 Skyraider attack aircraft and NAA T-28 Trojan trainers. Up until then, these two aircraft relied in over-the-side bailouts. The Skyraider was used heavily in Vietnam in low-level attacks, and the YANKEE seat undoubtedly saved many lives. After the death of Robert Stanley, the company withdrew from the escape system field and sold the YANKEE system license to Stencel, who in turn became part of Universal Propulsion Co. Inc. (UPCO), a division of B.F. Goodrich. Lockheed Aircraft purchased the license to build the Stanley upward ejection seats used in their F-104, U-2, A-12, and SR-71 Blackbird aircraft.

Stencel Stencel built the ejection seats for the McDonnell Douglas AV-8B Harrier and Northrop YF-17 fighter. Stencel purchased the license to build and sell the Stanley YANKEE escape system. Later, Stencel was merged into B.F. Goodrich's UPCO Division (Universal Propulsion Company).

Vultee Prior to becoming part of Convair, Vultee designed the nonpowered (gravity-type) ejection seat for the XP-54 Swoose Goose.

Weber Aircraft Weber Aircraft was probably the least well known of the ejection seat manufacturers and yet was one of the largest, having built over 3,000 seats. Some of the aircraft equipped with Weber ejection seats are as follows: the Boeing B-47 Stratojet (upward ejecting) and B-52 Stratofortress (upward ejecting); the Cessna T-37 trainer; the Douglas RB-66 Destroyer; the Convair F-102 Delta Dagger and F-106 Delta Dart; the Fairchild A-10 Thunderbolt II (Warthog) and Fairchild/Republic T-46A trainer; the General Dynamics F-16 Fighting Falcon; the

EJECT!

Glenn L. Martin Co. X-24 lifting body; the Grumman XF10F-1 Jaguar; the McDonnell F-101 Voodoo and F-15 Eagle; the Northrop M2F2 lifting body and HL-10 lifting body; the Lockheed YF-22 Raptor; the Republic F-105 Thunderchief; the Rockwell International B-1B Lancer; and ejection seats for several spacecraft. Weber Aircraft is still in business but no longer builds ejection seats.

Chapter Sixteen

THE FUTURE:
SAVE THE
ENTIRE AIRCRAFT?

Unlike the escape systems described in the previous chapters, Cirrus chose a completely different approach. The concept is simple: a large parachute is used to return the aircraft to the earth with the crew and passengers remaining within the aircraft. Obviously, though, developing this method was not as simple.

Cirrus Design SR20 General Aircraft

The Cirrus Design SR20 was a four-place, single-engine, fixed-landing-gear general aircraft of composite construction. The SR20 (R/N N200SR) was first flown from Duluth International Airport in Duluth, Minnesota, on March 31, 1995. The pilot for this flight was Norman Howell. In addition to its composite design, the SR20 had another unique feature: a side

Shown here is a Cirrus Design SR20, four-place composite aircraft. As standard equipment, the SR20 was equipped with an airborne Cirrus Airframe Parachute System (CAPS). *Cirrus Design*

control yoke for each of its two pilots.

Soon after its first flight, the presidents of Cirrus Design and Ballistic Recovery Systems (BRS) entered into a business relationship in which a whole-airframe recovery parachute system would become integral with the SR20, became standard delivery equipment, and was included in its basic price.

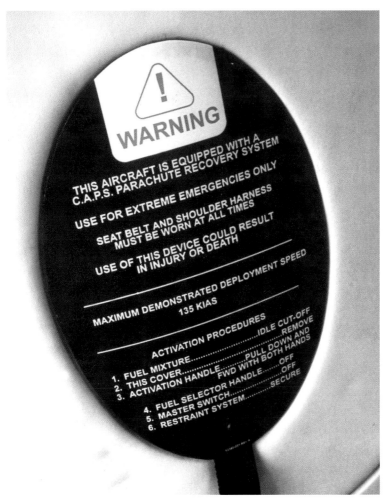

Activation of the CAPS occurred by pulling an overhead lever in the cockpit, which was covered by a guard, as shown. *Cirrus Design*

The major components of the recovery system came from BRS.

It is interesting to note that the original idea for recovering an entire airplane came from a Capt. M. Douade in 1913, utilizing a parachute canopy fabricated from Japanese silk. The SR20 whole-airframe parachute recovery system is called Cirrus Airframe Parachute System (CAPS).

The recovery system was complemented by a four-point seating harness and 26-g seats—the restraint harness and seat were designed to accept structural loads of 26 times the force of gravity—equipped with energy-absorbing cushions for each of the four places. CAPS was only intended to be used in the event of a life-threatening emergency, where CAPS deployment was determined to be safer than continued flight and landing. CAPS deployment was expected to result in loss of the airframe, and depending upon adverse external factors such as high deployment speed, low altitude, rough terrain, or very high wind conditions, deployment could result in serious injury or death to its occupants.

Eight airborne CAPS deployments were required to validate the system. These deployments were performed over a range of aircraft speeds from stall to maximum allowable, including flaps up and down and with the aircraft in a spin. Cirrus pilot Scott Anderson performed all of these tests on the original prototype aircraft (R/N N200SR). The prototype was not designed for a CAPS installation and thus required some modifications for these tests. In addition to the structural modifications, a "flight-test only" manual release system was installed. The airframe structural impact load testing was conducted in the factory, so the purpose of these airborne tests was to validate CAPS deployment only. Thus, after each CAPS test deployment, the pilot pulled the "flight-test only" release handle, which mechanically detached the parachute bridles from their three anchors.

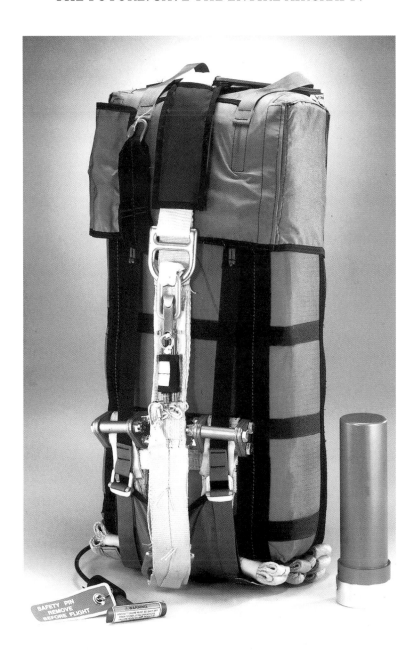

Shown here is the Ballistic Recovery System (BRS) parachute and tractor rocket for the Cirrus Design SR20. The recovery parachute was 55 inches in diameter. The cylindrical object to the right is the tractor rocket. *Ballistic Recovery System photo*

A flight-test base was established at Thermal, California. The CAPS deployment tests were performed nearby, over Ocotillo Wells, a desert-like area in Southern California, near the U.S.–Mexico border. This area was chosen for a number of reasons. It was a remote area, so the operation would not interfere with ground or airborne activity. The desert floor was below sea level, providing additional height for test pilot Anderson to do an over-the-side bailout, if required. The area also permitted off-roading, so each of the parachutes could easily be recovered. Another positive feature of this location was that it provided an area with rare inclement weather, so rain or storm delays would probably not be encountered.

After each test CAPS deployment, the recovery parachute was detached and the aircraft was flown back to the airport in Thermal, where a new CAPS parachute and tractor rocket were installed for the next test. Each of the eight tests was successful, and the flight-testing was completed in September, 1998.

The last of the CAPS tests was conducted at the Cirrus factory. One of these tests involved dropping an SR20 airframe at a height that would duplicate the rate of descent that could be expected during a CAPS recovery. The purpose of this—and additional testing—was to validate the ability of the airframe and seating structure and the aircrew's seating harness to work together to minimize harm to the aircrew. The seating and airframe structure testing were successfully completed in October 1998. Through the teamwork efforts of Cirrus Chief Engineer Paul Johnston and BRS Chief Engineer Tony Kasher, the Federal Aviation Administration granted certification to the SR20 under FAR Part 23.

How CAPS Works

Now let's look in detail at how CAPS operates. The luggage compartment in the SR20 is located in the rear of the cabin with the BRS parachute and tractor rocket located just aft of that on the upper aircraft centerline. The entire CAPS system weight is only 60 pounds. A handle in the roof of the cockpit mechanically activates a solid-fuel rocket tractor motor, which launches the 55-foot-diameter parachute within one second. The specifications for the recovery parachute contained several difficult requirements. To minimize its stored volume within the SR20, it had to withstand hydraulic pressure packing into a small container. The system had to be low cost and highly reliable.

Shown here are Paul Johnston, Cirrus chief engineer; Scott Anderson, Cirrus test pilot; and Gary Black, Cirrus flight-test engineer, at the Thermal, California, test site for CAPS. *Cirrus Design*

It also had to be a "smart" parachute—one that would quickly deploy at slow speeds, allowing for low-altitude emergency saves, but one that could withstand the opening loads at high speed. The key to the success of this project was the ingenious development by two BRS employees of a dynamic parachute reefing system, which was intended to slow the

Shown here is the prototype Cirrus Design SR20 after a test deployment of its parachute system. The white circle of light near the bottom of the parachute risers is the slider, having already performed its function of controlling the rate of parachute inflation. *Cirrus Design*

canopy opening in some circumstances and rapidly in others. These men were Bruce Case and Phil Kadlec, who persisted in demanding that BRS pay attention to their unusual idea.

By sheer creativity and ingenuity, Case and Kadlec went out on their own weekend time and repeatedly deployed a sliding-ring device that performed the functions required. This "slider," as it is now called, has enabled BRS to create ever-larger parachutes for ever-faster aircraft. Bruce Case also courageously performed the first in-air test deployments using the slider.

A tear-out strip was located along the outboard sides of the upper cockpit mold lines, allowing two forward bridles to be exposed. These bridles, together with the one rear bridle, provided a three-point suspension of the fuselage. Thus the aircraft was lowered to the ground, essentially in a normal horizontal flight attitude.

The first production aircraft was delivered in July 1999 and by May 2001, Cirrus had delivered 140 and had firm orders for 411 additional aircraft. In addition, Cirrus has developed a higher-horsepower version: the SR-22. In May 2001, Cirrus had delivered 40 SR-22s and had firm orders for over 200 more. This looks like a success story in the making.

GLOSSARY

AFB Air Force Base.

AGL Above ground level.

Aeroembolism Above 30,000 feet, gas bubbles may enter the circulatory system and form obstructions. This condition, known popularly as the bends, can lead to confusion or paralysis.

Altitude sickness This condition results from acute oxygen deficiency. From 13,000 to 35,000 feet in altitude, breathing oxygen will provide an adequate saturation of oxygen in the blood. Above that altitude, additional protection must be utilized. If not, the airman will experience hypoxia, which is seen as mild intoxication, followed by progressive loss of attention and judgment until unconsciousness occurs. Prolonged lack of oxygen may cause damage to the brain.

Center of gravity A point at which all the weight of an object can be considered concentrated.

Edwards Air Force Base The first known use of this 301,000-acre stretch of the Mojave Desert was in 1882, as a watering stop for the Atchison Topeka and Santa Fe Railroad. But no one made a determined effort to tame this expanse until the arrival of the Corum family, in 1910.

Muroc was first utilized by the military in September 1933, when a small advance party from March Field came to lay out and maintain bombing and gunnery targets. On June

21, 1940, Muroc Dry Lake was officially dedicated by the U.S. Army as Muroc Bombing and Gunnery Range. On December 8, 1949, the base took on its present name of Edwards Air Force Base.

G-force The force of attraction of the earth upon a body at sea level is stated as g. When standing still, we would then be in a 1G or +G condition. Changing velocity or speed is called acceleration. The axis or direction of acceleration is defined as follows:

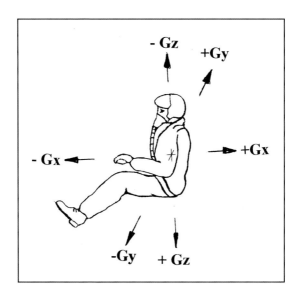

DESCRIPTION	SYMBOL
Eyeballs in	+Gx
Eyeballs out	-Gx
Eyeballs down	+Gz
Eyeballs up	-Gz
Eyeballs left	+Gy
Eyeballs right	-Gy

IFR Instrument flight rules is when visibility is less than three miles and/or the ceiling is 1,000 feet or less. Whenever both of these minimums are exceeded, you have VFR (visual flight rules) conditions.

KEAS Knots estimated air speed.

Kts Knots (nautical miles) per hour.

Mach Named after Austrian physicist Ernst Mach (1838–1916), who defined the ratio between the velocity of a moving object and the speed of sound.

An aircraft's Mach number equals: $\dfrac{\text{velocity of aircraft}}{\text{velocity of sound}}$

NAA North American Aviation, Inc., was a large aircraft company formed in 1935. Later it became part of Rockwell International, and later yet became part of Boeing Aerospace.

NAS Naval Air Station.

PSI Pounds per square inch.

USAAC United States Army Air Corps.

U.S. Air Force United States Air Force.

USMC United States Marine Corps.

USSR Union of Soviet Socialist Republics.

VFR Visual flight rules is defined when visibility exceeds three miles and/or the ceiling is 1,000 feet or more. When either of these conditions is not met, you have IFR (instrument flight rules) conditions.

V/STOL Vertical/short take off and landing.

BIBLIOGRAPHY

Ad Inexplorata. Air Force Flight Test Center History Office, via Edwards Air Force Base.

Aviation Week and Space Technology. August 2, 1993, and June 21, 1999.

B-1 Flight Manual NA-73-296 (AF74-0158A and AF74-0159A). Rockwell International, October 29, 1982.

B-58 Hustler News. Volume 1, Number 6. Convair Division of General Dynamics, May, 1961.

Brown, W. D. Parachutes. Great Britain: Sir Isaac Pitman and Sons, Ltd., 1951.

Compton's 1996 Interactive Encyclopedia. Compton's Multimedia, Inc., 1996.

Coyne, Kevin M. The Ejection Site. www.bestweb.net.

Groliers 1998 Multimedia Encyclopedia. Corel Corp, 1998.

Hay, Doddy. The Man in the Hot Seat. London: Collins of St. James Place, 1969.

Hegenwald, James. F. Jr., Harold L. Neumann, and Edward A. Murphy Jr. Aerial and Sled Testing of the B-70 Aircrew Escape Capsule. Prepared for presentation at the Annual Symposium of the Society of Experimental Test Pilots, Los Angeles, October 6–8, 1960.

Hegenwald, James F. Jr., Jerome F. Madden, and Paul R. Penrod. X-15 Research Aircraft Emergency Escape

System. Report 243 for the Advisory Group for
Aeronautical Research and Development, May 1959.

Los Angeles Skywriter. Volume XVII, No. 49. December 6,
1957.

Patton, R. E., Ph.D. A History of Developments in Aircrew
Life Support Equipment: 1797–1996. R. E. Patton: 1996.

Philpott, Byron. Eject! Eject! London: Ian Allan, Ltd., 1989.

Pierce, T. H. First to Jump. Volume XLII, No. 8. Raleigh,
North Carolina: The State, January 1975.

Poynter, Dan. The Parachute Manual. Santa Barbara, Ca.:
Para Publishers, 1984.

Ryan, Craig. The Pre-Astronauts. Annapolis, Md.: Naval
Institute Press, 1995.

Rocket Catapult Mark 1 Mod 0, NAVWEPS OP 2786. First
revision. The Chief of the Bureau of Naval Weapons,
June 1960.

Schiffer, Wolfgang. The History of German Aviation, The
First Aircraft. Military/Aviation History. Atglen,
Pennsylvania.

Sky Diver: The International Magazine of Parachuting.
April–June 1973.

Smith, J. Richard, and Eddie J. Creek. Jet Planes of the Third
Reich. Boylston, Massachusetts: Monogram Aviation
Publications.

Sweet, Harry E., Manager, Crew Escape Systems North
American Aviation Aircraft Division of Rockwell
International. Crew Module Systems Report NA-74-775.
October 23, 1974.

ACKNOWLEDGMENTS

Bill Adams, Gus Bateas, Gordon Cress, and John Shulansky
for photos and data on the Russian Zvezda K-36
ejection seat.

William Bagwell and Pete Williams for their escape stories
from the Douglas A-1 Skyraider using the Stanley
Aviation YANKEE system.

Dan Barry for historical support on the David Clark Company.

Bob Bashaw U.S. Navy/Ret. owner of Vintage Parachutes, for
photos of World War II parachutes.

Clinton Ray "Clint" Brisendine for his bailout story, and Ray
Bissell for his data loan on the Stanley encapsulated
seat used in the Convair B-58 Hustler.

Jim Boyer for his bailout stories from a Lockheed T-33
Silverstar and McDonnell Aircraft F-4 Phantom II, using
Martin-Baker ejection seats.

Lewellyn "Lew" Case, for his over-the-side bailout story from
the Martin B-26 Maurader, and David Giordano,
National Archives military records archivist, for
support of Case's bailout story.

William F. Chana, Rueben Snodgrass, and Gen. Chuck Yeager
on determining that the XP-81 was the first Convair
A/C equipped with an ejection seat.

Ken Collins and Mele Vojvodich Jr., for their ejection seat
bailout stories from a Lockheed A-12.

Scott Crossfield, Jerry Madden, and Harold Shapiro for their
photos and data support of the North American
Aviation X-15 ejection seat.

Bob DellaRovere for his artistic drawing support.

Sonia Dickey, archivist at The Mighty Eighth Air Force Heritage Center, for data on World War II bombing raids over Germany and photo support.

John Dzurica Sr., and John Dzurica Jr., for their encouragement and support in providing data, photos, and aid in research of Douglas Aircraft records.

Fred Erb of the Southern California Historical Aviation Foundation for early Northrop ejection seat history.

Mervin L. "Merv" Evenson and Gen. Richard V. Dick Reynolds, commander, Aeronautical Systems Center, Wright Patterson Air Force Base, for his story of ejecting and flying chase on a Rockwell International B-1A, ship number two bomber.

Lowell Ford and "Rocky" Rhodes (now deceased) for drawings and photos of the Vultee XP-54 Swoose Goose fighter.

Cecil A. Glass, Bob McIntyre, Bob Spear, and Hal Watson for providing historical background, detail design, data, photographs, and information on the operation of the rocket catapult and for providing Douglas Aircraft ejection seat photos and data.

Dave Greek and Norm Lefritz for human engineering data and flight-rules support.

Karen Hagar, executive secretary for communications at Lockheed.

Martin Aeronautics Co. and Mike Moore, software quality assurance engineering specialist, for providing photos and drawings of the Convair B-58 and F-111.

Helmuth Fredrick Hanson (now deceased), for his story of bailing out of a Boeing B-17F Flying Fortress, and Ann Easterling and Lt. David Lionberger of the Air Force History Center at Maxwell Air Force Base, for support of Fred Hanson's bailout story.

ACKNOWLEDGMENTS

John Henderson and Bill Simone for data on the North American Aviation B-45 Tornado, XP-86 Sabre, and XA2J-1 escape systems.

Del Holyland of Martin-Baker Aircraft Co. Ltd., for ejection seat photos and data.

Dan Johnson of Ballistic Recovery Systems, and Paul Johnston, Cindy Brown, and Chris Maddy of Cirrus Design Corp., for data, photos, and editorial help on the Cirrus SR20 recovery system.

Dean S. Jorgensen of Pioneer Aerospace Corp., for data and references on parachute design.

Don Kreis and Dave Wisted for the North American Aviation YF-107A ejection seat design story.

Tony Landis, for providing photos of the ejection seats used on the Lockheed   A-12 and SR-71 aircraft.

Ted Lida for data on Lockheed ejection seats history.

Denny Lombard of Lockheed Martin Skunk Works for providing photos of the Lockheed A/C and tips on other archivists.

Mike Lombardi, Boeing corporate historian, and Tom Lubbesmeyer, Boeing archivist, for providing data and photos from the Boeing Archives.

Lawrence E. Merritt, archivist/historian, McDonnell Aircraft/McDonnell Douglas/Boeing, St. Louis, for providing photos and drawings on the crew escape module McDonnell built for the Convair F-111, as well as photos of McDonnell aircraft.

Pat McGinnis, Boeing history archives, and Bill Hutchison, Boeing executive producer, for data and photos of Douglas aircraft.

Howard Mixon, military marketing manager of Irvin Aerospace, Inc., and Frank Chevrier, president of FXC Corp., for history and photos of automatic timed and barometric parachute deployment devices.

Clarence L. "Monty" Montgomery, Col. U.S. Air Force, ret.;
Louis Hughes, Lt. Col. U.S. Air Force, ret.; and Ken
Timpson, for their B-58 Hustler bailout stories using the
Convair ejection seat.

Douglas C. Nelson, director, AFFTC Museum, for data on the
Stanley YANKEE escape system and tips on locating
ejection seat users. Sigrid O'Dell, of Stanley Aviation,
for photo and data support on the YANKEE extraction
system. Bob Sadler, director, ACES II Program, and
Dick Higgins, manager, Hurricane Mesa Test Track,
both of Universal Propulsion Company, a division of
B.F. Goodrich, for data and photo support of the
Stanley Aviation YANKEE system, plus many tips on
historical sources of ejection seat components.

Brian Nicklas, museum specialist, Archives Division of the
National Air and Space Museum, for his extensive data
and photo support.

Dan Poynter of Para Publishing for guidance on this book,
providing photos, and tips on other parachute-related
sources.

Wayne Roberts, for providing photos and data on ejection
seats built by Weber Aircraft.

Russ Scott, for the story of his bailout from a North American
Aviation F-100 Super Sabre and for his tips on locating
escape system builders and users.

Society of Experimental Test Pilots for locating pilots who used
escape systems.

David Standish, for photos, data, and historical support on
the North American Aviation XB-70A Valkyrie
encapsulated ejection seat, Rockwell International
B-1A crew escape module, and ejection seats used in
the B-1B.

David Thigpen, for his bailout story from a General
Dynamics F-111 using its crew escape module.

ACKNOWLEDGMENTS

Crystal Tuttle, my patient granddaughter, who assisted me in
    looking through thousands of photographs to locate
    those pertinent to this book.
William A. Weaver, for his survival story from a Lockheed
    SR-71 Blackbird.
Alvin S. White, for his ejection story from a North American
    Aviation XB-70A Valkyrie.
Dr. James Young, AFFTC (Edwards Air Force Base) historian,
    for references and data support.

INDEX

248